Forgiveness Is

copyright@CN2022

ISBN: 9798364139160

Books In Print- Paperback,

All Rights Reserved. No portion of this book may be reproduced, stored in a retrieval system, or transmitted in any form or by any means, electronic, mechanical, photocopy, recording or other except for brief biblical quotations, without prior written permission of the author and publisher.

Scripture quotations referenced from the Holy Bible.

Forgiveness Is

Life Changing Stories from Las Vegas Chaplains

"To be a Christian means to forgive the inexcusable because God has forgiven the inexcusable in you." C. S. Lewis"

Colossians 3:13-14 "Bear with each other and forgive one another if any of you has a grievance against someone. Forgive as the Lord forgave you. And over all these virtues put on love, which binds them all together in perfect unity."

Luke 23:34 "And Jesus said, "Father, forgive them, for they know not what they do." And they cast lots to divide his garment

Matthew 18:22 Then Peter came to Jesus and asked, "Lord, how many times shall I forgive my brother who sins against me? Up to seven times?" 22 Jesus answered, "I tell you, not just seven times, but seventy-seven times!

copyright@CN2022

Foreword

"FORGIVENESS IS "

This was probably the most difficult book in this anthology to complete. Our authors had to dig deep and be very transparent in dealing with the writing process and memories that may not have been the most pleasant.
The blank pages were fighting the authors. Full writer's block occurred. Complete blankness at times.
What to write?
What to say?
What is the true meaning of forgiveness?
What is the benefit of forgiving?
Who must I forgive?
Who must I ask forgiveness from?
"Therefore, if you are offering your gift at the altar and there remember that your brother or sister has something against you, leave your gift there in front of the altar. First go and be reconciled to them; then come and offer your gift." Matthew 5:23-24
We all desire in our hearts to please God and be a faithful servant yet we cannot if we are living in disobedience by not forgiving. Not forgiving ourselves, not forgiving others, and not forgiving God for the trials and tribulations that come with life and living.
We are called to be mature Christians behaving in holiness and shining our lights so we can set the example for other believers and nonbelievers.
Examples of answers to these questions will be discovered while reading the personal stories of each author in this edition of our Five Part Chaplaincy Nevada "Faith Is " Anthology Series.
Take the time to explore each unique testimony and know that the writer's journey these authors walked was not taken alone. It's not easy to go back and look at the extraordinary incident of life that God has seen us through. It takes courage, grit and intestinal fortitude to stand up and reclaim the incidents of the past for God's glory.

* For our Good.
"And we know that all things work together for good to them that love God, to them who are the called according to His purpose." Romans 8:28
During this process God was ever present. The Holy Spirit guided them in their writings, and they are giving an account of their private testimonies of their choice to follow and serve Jesus Christ.
From our first class we determined no one would walk alone and I congratulate every Chaplain that crossed the finish line to present their personal stories in this book to the world.

Enjoy! Tamia Dow, Board Certified Chaplain, and Compiler

Forgiveness Is

Table of Contents

One: Forgive Like Jesus: Tamia Dow: P. 5

Two: Forgiveness Is Jesus: Victorya: P. 13

Three: Forgiveness Is a Process: Barry Mainardi: P.19

Four: The Weight of Forgiveness: Diane Rivera: P. 34

Five: Forgiveness & Memoirs: Estrellita Perry: P. 44

Six: Forgiveness Is My Legacy: Della Frank: P.54

Seven: Forgiveness Is a Fork in The Road: Shirley Lyons: P. 66

Eight: Are You Strong Enough to Forgive: Mike Puccio: P. 76

Nine: Forgiveness is Truly Loving Another: Susan Clark: P. 88

Ten: Forgiveness Is Love: Joann Hamilton: P. 99

Eleven: Forgiveness Is Selflessness: Randall Patterson: P. 111

Twelve: Forgiveness the Day My Eyes Really Opened: Laura Bjork: P: 123

Thirteen: Forgiving What You Can't Forget: Michelle Hatter: P. 134

Fourteen: True Forgiveness Is of The Heart: LaVenia Davis-Sandoval: P:140

Fifteen: Forgiveness Is Letting Go: Ingmar Joel Njus: P.149

Sixteen: Forgiveness Is the Ministry of Reconciliation: Beatrice Dyess: P. 159

BC Chaplain Tamia Dow

Tamia is a beloved child of God who serves God, her community, and her fellow (hu)man in many ways. She's a graduate from the University of Nevada Las Vegas (UNLV) with a Bachelors Degree in Criminal Justice, a veteran of the US Army, and a retired Las Vegas Metropolitan Police Department (LVMPD) Detective.
Tamia is an award-winning international best-selling author and an award-winning filmmaker who creates socially conscious faith affirming movies sharing her police experiences and dealing with current issues affecting our community.
Tamia is the compiler and coauthor of the Chaplaincy Nevada's book series which include; "Faith Is Inspiring Stories from Las Vegas Chaplains ", "Jesus Is Transforming Testimonies Of Las Vegas Chaplains ", "Love Is Heartwarming Memoirs from Las Vegas Chaplains " and "Hope Is Encouraging Chronicles from Las Vegas Chaplains".
Tamia's passion is to empower and educate people to live a life free from oppression and to live their life to their fullest calling.
She speaks and conduct trainings worldwide in the area of living a God planned life, Leadership, Domestic Violence and Human Trafficking Prevention and Awareness.
Tamia also coaches authors to complete their testimonies in book and/or screenplay format.
Tamia graduated from Kairos School of Ministry through the International Church of Las Vegas (ICLV) and does global police and community outreaches/missions.
Tamia is a Board-Certified Chaplain working with Veterans and First Responders, an Academy specialty instructor and a member of the Chaplaincy Board Consultants with the Messages of Faith Ministries, Chaplaincy Nevada.
She is a co-host and a Founding member of "Faith Is Live "the Messages of Faith Ministries monthly internet Talk Show which is now in its third season.
She serves as a Police Consultant on the Adopt A Cop Nevada (AACN) Advisory Board.

Tamia can be reached via :
https://linktr.ee/TamiaDow
IMDb.me/TamiaDow

† Forgive Like Jesus
By Tamia Dow

Don't let little things become big things. In this behavior the enemy rejoices.

"Be kind and compassionate to one another, forgiving each other, just as in Christ, God forgave you." Ephesians 4:32 (NIV)

Often times in life things will happen that don't necessarily go the way that we want them to. We have to decide how we are going to respond to them. How much energy were going to give to the disappointment and how we will move on from the disappointment.

Will we forgive the person that caused a disruption and continuing to be open to share an opportunity with another person? Would we not be penalizing others for the previous person's behavior?

I think of the times I have been invited to Church Conferences, film screenings, social events, and many other things and been asked to bring a friend or friends. I would invite a friend, or many times friends of mine as the host requested. I thought, what a blessing to be able to bless others.

I would announce it to my friends, text them, post on social media and sometimes make a personal phone call to invite them to participate in the event (that would be a blessing since most of the time there was a cost to attend the event and they would be attending at no cost). I truly thought I was being kind to invite other people to come when I didn't have to. I saw it as God's favor. The invitation was usually intended just for me, and other times for a few more dependable friends. Un-fortunately, some would say "yes, I will be there," often times saying they would bring friends or family members then they did not show up. I would be upset.

I was asked by promoters and event planners to assist in filling their events and the people I reached out to expecting them to attend ... did not. Not all mind you more showed up then not. Yet the no calls, no shows, no apologies these folks really grieved my heart. Common courtesy would dictate a call, text, some kind of a response.

I had to take this to God. And he reminded me of the parable of the wedding feast. Many people do not understand or realize the cost for the promoters and providers when it comes to event planning and because they themselves do not incur a financial part they value it less than if they paid out of their own pocket.

Therefore, while the planners and inviters were excited and eager to welcome their guest, the invited guest easily opted out without even properly notifying the host because they did not lose anything monetary by not showing up.

How does one remedy this and forgive the "No Call, No Show "for their disrespect and disregard of the invitation? The Lord reminded me "Many are called yet few are chosen." These people deselected themselves from a blessing.

I could not dwell too long on those who did not show. I celebrated those who did and told myself not to invite just anyone next time an opportunity presented itself. My lesson was to be more selective in who I invited. I let the Holy Spirit reveal who to invite to what opportunity.

This helped me to not to harbor unforgiveness towards those who did not bother to attend or even call me to tell me they were not planning to attend. The enemy uses little things like this to pit believers against one another. Our self-talk might say "He or She didn't do as I thought they should do so I am going to write them off."

This is unacceptable. No matter what they do or how the treat us, we must forgive them. So, I did, and I do. There will be another circumstance where I will feel someone did not do as I thought they should do. That is not for me to judge. We are all different and unique people. Just because we would do something a certain way does not mean someone else would do the same. I will forgive them and ask God to reframe the perceived offense to help me understand.

I pray "Lord help me see them through your eyes and to forgive and show love." I also ask the Holy Spirit if I am supposed to bring it up with the person (people) or to simply forgive them for my own mental health and peace of mind and move/choose more wisely in the future.

There are times to address it with your brother or sister in Christ and there are times to place it firmly in The Lord's hands so He can deal with their heart.

Let the Holy Spirit guide you.

We are called to forgive fully with love and appreciation in our heart. Sometimes, other people's bad behavior is God's protection. He is showing us ahead of time who is for us and who is against us. We must be wise in our affiliations and our associations. Wrong treatment sometimes happens to move us on and to awaken us to where and what God truly wants us to be, or do.

Sometimes we attempt to fit in in the wrong places, with the wrong people, in the wrong circumstances. Be mindful of your circle of friends.

"Do not be misled: "Bad company corrupts good character." 1 Corinthians 15:33 (NIV)

The Holy Spirit speaks to us, to our heart, to our minds, and to our spirit. We must be obedient and move on. Fear can keep us stuck.

Fear of the unknown. Fear of what will happen when we leave the situation. Also, pride can cause reluctance to have "them" (the perceived wrong doer) move us from what we believe we want. This may also contribute to us overstaying in the very place which God has already released us from.

In the end if we leave by our choice or by others actions, God will oversee it and work it together for our good. We are called to trust He will work it together for our good because He will.
"And we know that in all things God works for the good of those who love him, who have been called according to his purpose."
Romans 8:28 (NIV)

He wants us to be in place to best serve Him and move His will forward in this world. If we dwell too long in a place of unforgiveness looking too long at a closed door of perceived wrong, we may miss the blessings at the next-door God has for us. Often in the season we stand at that closed door we miss God's blessings and may be out of His will.
"For I know the plans I have for you," declares the Lord, "plans to prosper you and not to harm you, plans to give you hope and a future." Jeremiah 29:11 (NIV)

Do not stand too long at those closed doors. Forgive others because Christ has forgiven us. Walk into God's destiny for our lives. Christ's forgiveness is everlasting. He forgave us before we were even born. He knows all we will do, and all the choices we will be presented with. Free will is our gift. We can freely choose to follow Christ or to reject Him.

God gave us His Son. Jesus Christ became man for us. During His time on earth, He modeled forgiveness to us. He was hated and murdered. He even asked His Father (God) to release Him from His earthly pain yet in the end Jesus stayed the course and suffered the cross for us (that would be you too dear reader).

At any time, Jesus Christ could have said "Enough, let them die in their sin." Yet He continues to this day to advocate for us to the Father, to stand at the door of the unsaved person's heart like a gentleman knocking to be let in, to forgive us for our daily denial of Him and His sacrifice by our actions and inactions and He chooses "Love ".

Lack of Forgiveness and Love cannot occupy the same space.
We are called to Love.
"A new command I give you: Love one another. As I have loved you, so you must love one another. By this everyone will know that you are my disciples if you love one another." John 13:34&35 (NIV)

The Lord Jesus Christ set that example through His life on earth and His resurrection. We are forgiven. Over and over again. 70 times 7. There is nothing we can do that if we ask for The Lord's forgiveness, that He would not forgive for us.

So Christian, Christ follower, what is it that someone could possibly do that you cannot forgive them for?

Model King Jesus. Follow His instruction in the Lord's Prayer given in the book of. Matthew Chapter 6. *"But if you do not forgive others their sins, your Father will not forgive your sins."*
Mathew 6:15 (NIV)

Forgive so that you too will be Forgiven and in right standing with Our God.
Glory to God!

✝

BC Chaplain Victorya

Victorya is a licensed Minister through the State of Nevada and Clark County Ministers License to Perform Marriages. Basic Chaplaincy Certification & Academy Training Development & Programmer. She is a Christian author published on both Amazon & Barnes Noble. Author of Chosen 15 Minutes with Jesus & Born Again. She co-authored the book Broken Wings Wounded Hearts with her 4 sisters.

In 2021 she was named the Winter Book Award Recipient and received The Pinnacle Book Achievement Award from the National Association of Book Entrepreneurs for Best Books in Christian Category for Chosen 15 Minutes with Jesus.

Victorya is an Invocator for CC Commissioners, City of LV Council meetings, and previously the CCSD Board Trustees. She is a graduate from mentor training with Hope for Prisoners ReEntry Program, a former S.NV. Community Gang Taskforce Coordinator, and a CCDC METRO Volunteer Program, a National Day of Prayer event coordinator. A former member Member of S. NV. Mental Health Coalition, Subcommittee member of CIT (Crisis Intervention Training), Jail Aftercare Program, Mental Health Court. LVMPD CIT Graduate 07, a Leadership & Resiliency Graduate, CLV CERT graduate, The 5 Critical Disciplines Certificate Graduate 2010. SNV Community Gang Taskforce GRT Handbook on Gangs Co-Instructor graduate. Courts Catalyzing Change member-Mental Health Sub-Chair, Faithbase subcommittee.Co-Founder ChallengeKADS Sports Association. 4th degree Black Belt Taekwondo. Victoria is the founder of NAFD and has worked in education for over 20 yrs co-sponsored with CCSN Cont. Ed. program/ CCSN Welfare to Work programs 1995-97, UNLV division of Educational Outreach from 1997 to present. Completed Chaplains Academy in religious studies 2013. In 2015 she was Awarded Lifetime Achievement Recognition for her work from the NV State Governors Office, US Senatorial, US House of Representatives, US House of Congress, and partnered organizations.

www.victorya.net

† Forgiveness Is Jesus

By Victorya

Then Peter came to Him and said, "Lord, how often shall my brother sin against me, and I forgive him? Up to seven times?" Jesus said to him, "I do not say to you, up to seven times, but up to seventy times seven." Matthew 18:21-22

Forgiveness has always been huge for me. It isn't because I believe that a person should harm another person physically, or emotionally, or because the harm that was done should be instantly forgotten, nor do I believe that we should immediately become best friends after the injury just so another individual can test our Christianity 70 x 7, plus no-one person will ever sincerely escape the damages caused, as God knows all things. Forgiveness is huge for me because it is what Jesus the Son of Almighty God asks of each one of us.

The day I met Christ He asked, "can you forgive". Though forgiveness can be a very tough request to consider, it is asking us to let go of an offense that deeply hurt us, and for some the unforgiveness has already been detrimental, and deeply rooted within their very own essence of existence. Can a human-being actually forgive, does the forgiveness remove all the pain in the manner of a miracle? That would depend. It depends upon the person being asked or merely contemplating the idea of suggestion, or it could depend upon the person who is actually asking. Jesus Himself is the miracle that can do all things in our lives, which includes wiping away our unforgiveness in the blink of an eye if we agree, or over time, just as He sees fit to handle the situation for it to work as best as He determines in our lives.

All I know is that at one time in my life, had any person in this world regardless of family, friend, priest, or pastor asked me to forgive another's deeply cutting transgression against myself then the answer would have been a resounding No. However, if that person is Jesus of Nazareth, Jesus the Galilean, Jesus the Son of God, Jesus the Redeemer, Jesus the Prince of Peace, Jesus the Messiah, and on, then the only answer possible from me would be a decisive, Yes Jesus.

As I lay awake one early morning, the sun was shining brightly through the bedroom curtains but yet you could see the shadow of the tree branches moving from pillar to post, the breezy air making the leaves seem as if they were dancing, and my mind began to examine the ways of which to tell a story of forgiveness, and the best way to explain it from my perspective. As I thought about this, I decided to ask Jesus what He thought would be best after all my perspective and His reality could be as far as the East is from the West, or I could just be over rationalizing it.

The longer I lay there my thoughts soon turned to prayers, and as my eyes roamed the room I caught hold of the picture hanging on the wall, the framed picture of Christ bending down and writing in the sand. Now most of us know the story behind the writing of the sand and if you don't, I'll be happy to share.

"The teachers of the law and the Pharisees brought in a woman caught in adultery. They made her stand before the group and said to Jesus, 'Teacher, this woman was caught in the act of adultery. In the Law Moses commanded us to stone such women. Now what do you say?' They were using this question as a trap, in order to have a basis for accusing him. But Jesus bent down and started to write on the ground with his finger." (John 8:3-6). The point of the Pharisees' exercise, however, was not to establish her guilt or innocence but to trap Jesus in a no-win situation. The religious authorities set a trap, believing Jesus would either be pressured to stone the woman or challenge their authority and, by implication, the law of God. Defying the authorities would have appeared rebellious and sinful, even though they were distorting Jewish law. What mattered most to the Scribes and Pharisees, however, was not right and wrong but humiliating Jesus and reasserting their authority among His followers. The accusers "kept on questioning him" as He stooped there, so Jesus "straightened up and said to them *'Let any one of you who is without sin be the first to throw a stone at her.'" (John 8:7)* Then, He stooped again to write something on the ground. This time, *(John 8:9) And they which heard it, being convicted by their own conscience, went out one by one, beginning at the eldest, even unto the last: and Jesus was left alone, and the woman standing in the midst."*

There has been so much speculation over centuries and decades as to what Jesus wrote in the sand, and many opinions given, however there is no factual historic evidence as to what the exact writing was, and therefore any theory or answer is either rooted in one of three responses 1. opinion 2. conjecture, or 3. Jesus. Any born again believer has complete access to the throne through prayer to ask anything, and the Lord answers us in His way usually according to the circumstance that we are laying before Him.

As I continued to reflect upon the picture I asked, "Lord what were you writing in the sand?" As I continued to listen for an answer, His reply suddenly came over me, invading my senses. He reminded me of the Pharisees trying to trick Him and punish a woman for her sins all at one time, and in His benevolence, His humanity, His Spiritual adoration, He said, *"I desire mercy, not sacrifice, Hosea 6:6"* and I realized at that very moment the woman was being used as the trick, and deliberately as the sacrifice to dismantle Christ and His followers. *"This is My commandment, that you love one another, just as I have loved you. John 15:12-13' 'Be kind and compassionate to one another, forgiving each other, just as in Christ God forgave you. Ephesians 4:32"*

At that moment I fully realized what the writing in the sand was, and this message given as an answer from Him over to me for a better understanding. But then I asked again, what did you write in the sand while they were wanting to sacrifice and stone the woman, all the while using her against you for the purpose of your destruction; much more than hers?

The answer written in the sand: "Forgive."

The answer was so clear to me as Jesus answers are always specific, and He always aligns His every spoken word with scripture, and as always, the Lord's desire for mercy and forgiveness in our lives and in the lives of all those whom we formulate relationships with, or just the strangers we come into contact with. Whatever the offense, even if we are the sacrifice, we must forgive.

The thought of Jesus being in the midst of that circumstance, while He was completely aware of His surroundings, the people, the religious leaders whom He knew were compelled to see Him destroyed, and the woman, sinful, however her being the opportunity to be used as the sacrifice to bring Jesus down is so poignant, because it's so wretched, so sorrowful, and so touching a combination, that the impression He would leave upon the minds and hearts of those he loves would be to...."Forgive."

Jesus Is Forgiveness~

BC Chaplain Barry Mainardi

Chaplain Barry graduated from the University of Dayton.
He served with the U.S. Army as an Airborne Jumpmaster/Instructor Pilot and served in two areas of combat including Vietnam. He received an Honorable Discharge at the rank of Captain.
Chaplain Barry is an Ordained Board Certified ("B.C.") Chaplain with Chaplaincy Nevada, serving as Director of Administration and Member/Past chair/Past Vice Chair of the Chaplaincy Advisory Board;
FREE International Las Vegas Representative; Las Vegas Mayor's Faith Based Initiative –
Human Trafficking Co-Chair; Clark County School District Human Trafficking Prevention Resource.
Empowerment Begins with Knowledge (EBK) Lead Editor; Las Vegas Coalition Against Trafficking (LVCAT) Co-Founder; International Coalition Against Trafficking (ICAT) Co-Founder; Rebuilding Every City Around Peace (RECAP); So. NV Human Trafficking Task Force (METRO) Education Committee; NV Child Abuse Prevention (CSAP); NV Coalition to Prevent the Commercial Sexual Exploitation of Children Committees (CSEC); NV Volunteers
Active in Disaster (NV-VOAD) Member; and serves as a Las Vegas METRO Volunteer since 2004.

My gratitude is extended to "GotQuestions.org" for their numerous articles and scripture on "Forgiveness". There are instances that the wording in the research documents provided by "GotQuestions.org" were so clear and concise, that I included various paragraphs verbatim in an effort to assist the reader with understanding that Forgiveness is a Process.

8635 W. Sahara Ave, #110 (702) 523-3052
Las Vegas, NV 89117 wsnetwork@AOL.COM

† Forgiveness Is a Process
By Barry Mainardi

I have a personality that does not respond easily to a "direct order" unless there is a reason or philosophy to support that "demand". The good news is, when God gives us an "Order", there is always a reason or explanation to support His Command, but it takes an effort to research and understand the "why". This is the reason why we have the Holy Spirit to assist us when we are reading the Bible.

I have been researching the meaning of forgiveness for 7 years. On the surface, the requirement to "forgive" seems simple enough:

• *Ephesians 4:32 (NIV) – "Be kind and compassionate to one another, forgiving each other, just as in Christ, God forgave you"*

… but is Forgiveness that simple? The key is, understanding under what conditions did "… God forgave you"?

What Forgiveness IS and IS Not

Let us begin by discussing what forgiveness IS NOT:

Forgiveness does not mean it is forgotten. Forgetting means He is not remembering to condemn us.

• *Romans 8:1 – "Therefore, there is now no condemnation for those who are in Christ Jesus,"*

The phrase "forgive and forget" can be misleading. To forget does not mean that a person who has been wronged develops some kind of sanctified amnesia. Yet, it is possible for us who have suffered to forgive and also to forget, as long as the biblical definition of forget is our definition.

In the Bible, remembering and forgetting do not have to do with retention of information in the brain. For instance, Gensis 8:1 (below) does not imply or state that God forgot about Noah. God is all knowing and ever present. He did not misplace him and "just remembered" to check on him. No, the biblical concept of remembering has to do with "choosing to act," and forgetting means "refusing to act" on the basis of something. When the Bible says God "remembered" Noah, it means that God chose to act on Noah's behalf at that time.

- *Genesis 8:1 – "But God remembered Noah and all the wild animals and the livestock that were with him in the ark, and he sent a wind over the earth, and the waters receded."*

Forgiveness does not eliminate all consequences here on Earth. We may suffer consequences for our sin(s) even if we are forgiven by God.

- *Hebrews 12:5-6 – "5 And have you completely forgotten this word of encouragement that addresses you as a father addresses his son? It says, 'My son, do not make light of the Lord's discipline, and do not lose heart when he rebukes you, 6 because the Lord disciplines the one he loves, and he chastens everyone he accepts as his son.'"*
- *Proverbs 6:27 "Can a man scoop fire into his lap without his*

clothes being burned?"

Forgiveness is not a feeling. We are committed to "pardon" the offender when the forgiveness process is completed. Negative feelings, bitterness and anger against an offender may reduce or fade in the future even without forgiveness being extended.
I believe that psychology was wrong when taught that "forgiveness" is one-sided, that reconciliation is unnecessary, and the purpose of this so-called unilateral forgiveness is to free the offended person of feelings of bitterness.

Forgiveness is not selfish. We do not forgive others for our own satisfaction or as a means to reduce stress in our lives. We forgive because of our Love of God and gratitude for our own forgiveness.
• *Psalm 119:36 – "Turn my heart toward your statutes and not toward selfish gain."*
• *Philippians 2:3 – "Do nothing out of selfish ambition or vain conceit. Rather, in humility value others above yourselves,"*
• *James 3:16 – "For where you have envy and selfish ambition, there you find disorder and every evil practice."*

Forgiveness is not the immediate or automatic restoration of trust. Rebuilding trust can only begin after the true Forgiveness Process is complete, which includes confession and repentance. A good friend, Pastor and Chaplain Dauda Presley gave me the following analogy of trust broken and the trust rebuilding process: "Trust is like a large bucket filled with trust-water that is spilled. In order to refill that bucket with trust-water, it takes many "communion cups" of water … and that takes time, assuming the trust-water does not spill again." But we must be prepared to "walk away" when we run out of "communion cups as it is written:

• *Proverbs 14:7 – "Stay away from a fool, for you will not find knowledge on their lips."*
• *Luke 16:10-12 clearly warns us - 10 "Whoever can be trusted with very little can also be trusted with much, and whoever is dishonest with very little will also be dishonest with much. 11 So if you have not been trustworthy in handling worldly wealth, who will trust you with true riches? 12 And if you have not been trustworthy with someone else's property, who will give you property of your own?"*
• *1 Corinthians 4:2 – "Now it is required that those who have been given a trust must prove faithful."*

Forgiveness is not a private, individual, or solitary act. It is a Process, or Partnership between the offended and the offender. We will discuss the importance of God's requirements later in this chapter. God's forgiveness of us and our forgiveness of others are not two separate, unrelated issues of forgiveness. They are vitally linked. It is essential for us to understand that confession and repentance are essential to the completion of the Forgiveness Process.

• *2 Corinthians 2:5 – "Forgiveness for the Offender: If anyone has caused grief, he has not so much grieved me as he has grieved all of you to some extent—not to put it too severely."*

- *Luke 17:3-4, "So watch yourselves. 'If your brother or sister sins against you, rebuke them; and if they repent, forgive them. Even if they sin against you seven times in a day and seven times come back to you saying, 'I repent,' you must forgive them.'"*
- *John 20:23, "If you forgive anyone's sins, their sins are forgiven; if you do not forgive them, they are not forgiven."*

What IS Forgiveness - What it takes to Forgive

The key condition or requirement to forgiveness is Repenting. Let us begin discussing the "repenting" requirement of forgiveness by quoting an essential scripture:

As is written in *Luke 23:34, Jesus said on the cross, "Father, forgive them, for they do not know what they do."*. His request for forgiveness was an opened ended request to the Father to be activated for those who Believe in Jesus and repented.

Let us begin with the definition of Forgiveness. An excellent definition of forgiveness is found in the book Unpacking Forgiveness by Chris Brauns:

"God's forgiveness: A commitment by the one true God to pardon graciously those who repent and believe so that they are reconciled to him, although this commitment does not eliminate all consequences.

General human forgiveness: A commitment by the offended to pardon graciously the repentant from moral liability and to be reconciled to that person, although not all consequences are necessarily eliminated."

Our Intimacy with God is dependent on our forgiveness of others, and our forgiveness of others is an example of God's forgiveness of us. We must understand God's forgiveness of us if we are to offer forgiveness to others that reflects God's forgiveness. Unfortunately, the word "forgiveness" is accepted "psychological freedom" and not "freedom from sin".

When you are reading the scripture below, it is important for us to understand the phrase, "… as the Lord forgave you." As I pointed out several times in my article, our Lord forgave those who repented and believed in Him, no matter how much time it took for "sinners" to understand this requirement.
- *Matthew 6:12* – *"And forgive us our debts, as we also have forgiven our debtors."*
- *Ephesians 4:32* – *"Be kind and compassionate to one another, forgiving each other, just as in Christ God forgave you."*
- *Colossians 3:13* – *"Bear with each other and forgive one another if any of you has a grievance against someone. Forgive as the Lord forgave you."*

It is important that focus on the words "confess" and "repent" because without that requirement, the forgiveness process cannot be completed. The offended person MUST offer forgiveness, but the "sinner" or offender must receive it through confessing and repenting. The relationship will be reconciled when that requirement is fulfilled. If we are unwilling to forgive others, then we become part of the problem in that we are refusing to allow others to enjoy the Blessings offered by God.

• *1 John 1:9 - "If we confess our sins, he is faithful and just and will forgive us our sins and purify us from all unrighteousness".*

God is willing to forgive any time we confess and repent our sins. In fact, he continuously facilitates or gives us opportunities to confess and repent so we can receive forgiveness. But the decision to come to Him is ours, which is why He gave us Free Will.

• *2 Peter 3:9 – "The Lord is not slow in keeping his promise, as some understand slowness. Instead, he is patient with you, not wanting anyone to perish, but everyone to come to repentance."*

If repenting is required to forgive and only the Father knows what is in our hearts, how can we forgive?

Obviously, we do not know what is in the heart of others, but God knew us before we were borne. There are many scriptures that testify to this fact, as I quoted below:

• *Psalm 139:1-4, "You have searched me, Lord, and you know me. 2 You know when I sit and when I rise; you perceive my thoughts from afar. 3 You discern my going out and my lying down; you are familiar with all my ways. 4 Before a word is on my tongue you, Lord, know it completely."*

It is important to realize that Forgiveness is a Process, not a solitary act. If the participants in the Forgiveness Process do not act as intended by Jesus on the cross, the process will not be completed, and forgiveness will not be granted by God.

Can we truly forgive someone by ourselves or are we offering forgiveness? Let's examine a scripture that I introduced at the beginning of my article: *Ephesians 4:32 (NIV) – "Be kind and compassionate to one another, forgiving each other, just as in Christ, God forgave you."* The key is, "…just as in Christ, God forgave you." God will forgive us if we satisfy two essential prerequisites; (1) we must repent and (2) we must believe that Jesus is our Lord and Savior. As a result, forgiveness must be a Process or Partnership consisting of two "parties" and the "Judge":

Forgiveness Offering Stage – The offended party Offers Forgiveness to the offender

We are required to offer forgiveness. Many scriptures support this "demand" several of which are stated in this article. However, a key scripture needs repeating. *Ephesians 4:32 (NIV) – "Be kind and compassionate to one another, forgiving each other, just as in Christ, God forgave you."* That phrase is key to the meaning of forgiveness. We must offer forgiveness and that offer is never withdrawn or rescinded. That is our only responsibility in the "Forgiveness Offering Stage".

The Forgiveness Offer may require direct communications with the offender and offended in a neutral environment. The objective is to discuss the details of the challenge or problem from both points of view.

Forgiveness Receiving Stage - The offender Receives the Forgiveness offer.

The offender must decide (Free Will) to accept or receive the Forgiveness offer. Failure to receive the Forgiveness Offer does not negate or cancel the Forgiveness Offer. We must follow Jesus's example on the cross to offer forgiveness to those who Believe in Jesus and repent. It is not up to us to determine when or if that happens.

• *Mathew 18:15-18, 15 "If your brother or sister[b] sins, [c] go and point out their fault, just between the two of you. If they listen to you, you have won them over. 16 But if they will not listen, take one or two others along, so that 'every matter may be established by the testimony of two or three witnesses.'[d] 17 If they still refuse to listen, tell it to the church; and if they refuse to listen even to the church, treat them as you would a pagan or a tax collector."*

God (The Judge) – Knows what is in the hearts of everyone and Judges according to His foreknowledge and His Will. He established the Rules and explained them through various Scriptures in our Bible. However, we have the Free Will to research His Word to achieve an understanding of the Forgiveness Process.

I have heard Christians say, "I forgave him so I can move on." This philosophy violates the true meaning and process of forgiveness.

That is not the meaning of forgiveness. It is important to understand that forgiveness offered and available is not the same as forgiveness given, received, and transacted. This is where the word forgiveness on its own with no qualifier is often used differently from, and beyond, how God's Word uses it.

We tend to call the attitude of forgiveness, being willing to forgive, just the same as the actual transaction of true forgiveness. That is, in popular thinking, as long as a person is open to granting forgiveness, he has already forgiven. But this broad definition of forgiveness short-circuits the process of confession and repentance. Forgiveness offered and forgiveness received are entirely different, and we don't help ourselves by using a catch-all word for both.

Should we forgive a person who does not confess his sin and is not repentant?
While we must not harbor bitterness in our hearts or repay evil for evil, we should make sure we follow God's lead and not extend the act of forgiveness to the unrepentant. In short, we should withhold forgiveness from those who do not confess and repent. However, it is essential and required by God that we extend the offer of forgiveness and maintain an attitude of readiness to forgive.
• *Hebrews 12:15 – "See to it that no one falls short of the grace of God and that no bitter root grows up to cause trouble and defile many."*
• *1 Peter 3:9 - Do not repay evil with evil or insult with insult. On*

the contrary, repay evil with blessing, because to this you were called so that you may inherit a blessing.

Stephen, even as he was being stoned to death, illustrates the principle extending the offer of forgiveness. Echoing Jesus' words from the cross, Stephen prays, "Lord, do not hold this sin against them. See Acts 7:60 below. These words show a definite willingness to forgive, but they do not indicate a completed transaction of forgiveness. Stephen simply prayed that God would forgive his murderers. Stephen held no bitterness, and, when and if his murderers repented, he wished them to be forgiven—what a wonderful example of
loving our enemies and praying for those who persecute us.
• *Acts 7:60 – "Then he fell on his knees and cried out, 'Lord, do not hold this sin against them.' When he had said this, he fell asleep."*
• *Matthew 5:44 – "But I tell you, love your enemies and pray for those who persecute you,"*

The Bible commands what could be confusing to some Christians in Romans 12:20. There is nothing Biblical that demands we automatically forgive our enemies (or trust them). Rather, we are to love them and work for their good.
• *Romans 12:20 - On the contrary: "If your enemy is hungry, feed him; if he is thirsty, give him something to drink. In doing this, you will heap burning coals on his head."*

Forgiveness should not be given prematurely, without the

prerequisites of confession and repentance, because both the offender and offended parties will not be dealing with the truth. If the offender doesn't acknowledge the sin, then the offender really does not understand what it means to be forgiven. In the long run, bypassing confession or repentance doesn't help the offender to understand the significance of sin, and it precludes a sense of justice, causing the offended person to battle even more against bitterness.

Important Points to Remember

Some of us have been "taught" to forgive immediately because that is what Jesus wants. Some of us have been taught to forgive because we will "feel better". However, Forgiveness is a Process that must be completed. Forgiveness is not just about the "offended". It is about being released from sin that only can be achieved by confessing and repenting. God demands that we offer forgiveness to everyone who sins against us and accept forgiveness to those who repent no matter how much time elapses. Our offer has no expiration date.

There is a difference between offering forgiveness and the act of forgiveness. The difference is confessing and repenting. Jesus' forgiveness request to the Father on the cross and Stephen's request as he was being stoned represents the "Forgiveness Offering Stage". Here are some key guidelines that God set for us to allow us to participate in the Forgiveness Process:

➢ We must acknowledge that evil exists
- Romans 12:9 Love in Action – "Love must be sincere. Hate what is

evil; cling to what is good."

➤ The Lord says, "It is mine to avenge". Therefore, bitterness revenge, grudges, or retaliation destroys Forgiveness.

• *Romans 12:19 – "Do not take revenge, my dear friends, but leave room for God's wrath, for it is written: 'It is mine to avenge; I will repay, says the Lord.'"*

➤ Always be ready to offer and receive forgiveness

• *Luke 17:3-4 – "3 So watch yourselves, if your brother or sister[a] sins against you, rebuke them; and if they repent, forgive them. 4 Even if they sin against you seven times in a day and seven times come back to you saying, 'I repent,' you must forgive them."*

➤ Always trust God to give you the strength to overcome evil with good, even to love and feed an enemy

• *Romans 12:20-21 - 20 On the contrary: "If your enemy is hungry, feed him; if he is thirsty, give him something to drink. In doing this, you will heap burning coals on his head." 21 Do not be overcome by evil but overcome evil with good.*

Remember that God has instituted governing authorities, and part of their God-given role is to be "God's servants, agents of wrath to bring punishment on the wrongdoer".

• *Romans 13:4 - For the one in authority is God's servant for your good. But if you do wrong, be afraid, for rulers do not bear the sword for no reason. They are God's servants, agents of wrath to bring punishment on the wrongdoer.*

My final thoughts…

The timing for our book was definitely directed by the Holy Spirit. The years of frustration I was experiencing on "the meaning of forgiveness" was limiting my growth with Jesus. I knew I was missing something, and I thank our Lord for opening my heart to receive His Guidance.

The answers to "What Is Forgiveness" were in my possession but as the expression suggests, "I was too close to the forest to see the trees." That's what happens when I do not "give it to God".
• *James 1:5 – "If any of you lacks wisdom, you should ask God, who gives generously to all without finding fault, and it will be given to you."*

I pray that everyone looks to our Lord for understanding and direction as we continue our search to seek His Truth.
• *Proverbs 3:5 – "Trust in the Lord with all your heart and lean not on your own understanding."*

✝

BC Chaplain Diane Rivera

Healthcare administration has been my line of duty for many years, now part of the Local Teamster union 986 and looking forward towards retirement, so that I can work full time at the Ministry. Since relocating to Las Vegas after 4 -years in Michigan, 2014, I have been part of the assembly "Centro Cristiano El Shaddai"and the sister church "Casa de Restauracion " where my functions have been as Assistant Pastor. . I completed 3- years of Theology at the "instituto Biblico Emmanuel" 2014-2017 Magna cum Laude. A Director of Christian Education, and Instructor for Chaplaincy within my church "Instituto Biblico Emmanuel.

I was ordained as a Chaplain 2017 with MOFM and graduated as a Sr. Chaplain 2018. I became an Ordained Pastor with my church in 2019.

I'm looking forward to obtaining a BC Chaplain in 2022. My greatest title, though the proudest I've been being a servant of the Lord. My heart cries for the lost and the hurting. I've been part of the Adopt-a -cop board, West Care, Hope Hospital, Rescue Mission, Teaching O.T & N.T with the Women's

† The Weight of Forgiveness
By Diane Rivera

Every one of us has found ourselves to have been hurt by another person's words or actions. Maybe your best friend forgot your birthday, you were criticized or abused by your parents, bullied as a child, or your spouse had an affair. Whether a big or small offense, it hurts to be wronged and keeping score only grows a deeper root of unforgiveness.

Hebrew 12:15 NIV "See to it that no one falls short of the Grace of God and that no bitter root grows up to cause trouble and defile many."

You see, The Weight of unforgiveness is real!!
My Name is Diane Rivera, I entered the world on Nov 22, 1960, during a cold winter at the Lincoln Medical Hospital in Bronx N.Y. Let me share what was "cool" in the 60's, afros, bell-bottoms, go-go boots, miniskirts, hippies with `` Peace & Love". Every lady wanted to be like "Twiggy" the model, and of course there was Beatlemania.

My Mother Marie Cruz, a beautiful woman of honey tone completion, very long, thick, beautiful black hair, was the only girl out of 4 boys in her family; being protected with a beautiful display of sibling love & respect all the way the through their adult lives. My mother and her brothers were raised in a Christian home. I remember Sunday mornings rain, snow, or shine grandma would pick us up for Sunday School. Both sets of my maternal grandparents & great grandparents always made sure my siblings and I knew the love of God the Father, His Son Jesus Christ, and the Holy Spirit. Grandma was a proud proclaimed volun-told grandmother. Oftentimes, she would have us sing a song, "It's me, it's me-oh…Lord standing in the need of prayer "(of course, we also sang the Spanish version).

My Father, on the other hand, was not quite so gentle. Although not great in stature, his presence was very intimidating. I don't remember him smiling other than when he was drunk, and then he became very volatile. Hearing the front door open each day when he came from work was the greatest torment for me. I would shake uncontrollably a fear that would overpower me. I would glance at my brother Kiki; his eyes would tell me he was scared too. My oldest brother was our protector. Only God knows how many times he experienced the wrath of my father. I was crying out to God and praying to the Lord please take him away, let him die!

One late night the front door opened, we were all in bed, dad walked into the kitchen, I quickly jumped out of bed and laid down on the floor of my dark bedroom with the door cracked open enough to see what he was doing. He got a pot from the kitchen cabinet, tuned on the faucet and I could see the heat as he filled the pot, and placed it on the stove. He walked to the bedroom. I thought to myself, why is he boiling water? It was pretty late and everyone else was asleep. I'm sure there was also some dinner left for him. He returned to the kitchen removing the pot from the stove. With pot in hand, he walked back to the bedroom, it was not long before we heard her scream… He threw hot water on my mother, after that horrible heart-breaking scream, my memory became vague. I don't remember if she said anything the next day or remained quiet.

Oftentimes, more than I care to remember, my brother and I bore my dad's physical abuse, as did my mom. He would use the leather belt buckle, horse whip, even his fist to display his wrath and anger. At a very tender age, I believed I could not be more than 8-9 years old at the time, when he punched me so hard, I was out cold with a black eye for the next few days. I asked myself, did anyone ever wonder what happened to me, as I looked at an old photo of myself. It was a reminder of Easter Sunday with my sister, Jennie, I am wearing a beautiful navy-blue sailor dress, easter bunny in hand and a fading black eye. So, as you can imagine the sense of security was stripped away at a very young age, and from there came the insecurities and low self-esteem. I had a long struggle with seeing value in myself I was seeking love and security and so I married at a very young age. He was tall a 6'2 named Angel (only by name) and by the age of 15-yrs. I had my first child. I don't remember when the abuse started. However, it progressed from verbal to physical abuse. I was being

punched, choked, and kicked as if I was worthless, and he spoke "You're Lucky to be with me, nobody would ever want you!!!" he would say and I believed him. I was being molded to accept, and to be quiet and submissive. I asked myself; what happened to me? How on earth did I find myself with this person that demanded obedience and loyalty by beating the very life out of me?
I wanted to escape but felt trapped. Maybe he was right, who would care? I was a 19-year-old with 3 small children, and so I kept silent. Someone once said, "when one's lost, I suppose it's good advice to stay where you are, until someone finds you".

You see, guilt is a powerful emotion that changes how you look, react, and respond to situations in life. I was so embarrassed I was afraid to tell anyone and oftentimes blaming myself. Was this how my mother felt? Would God ever forgive me? For 13- years my husband, as my father, would make me shake with fear. I could hear him coming as he would" burn rubber" on his way home announcing his arrival.

I see that little girl now, a young woman broken, and beaten. The little girl from her dad. The young woman from her husband. The little girl in me screamed, "I didn't do it!! The young woman cries out, "why are you doing this?" Two men created by God to protect and love me were the cause of my fear and pain. The last night of my abuse came, and he was drunk. I don't remember what I said or did but that he locked the three children in their bedroom right across from ours and dragged me to our bedroom, closed the door and beat me, I felt like this was my last day on earth. I was on the floor being stomped and kicked with no sound coming out of me, all I could think of was "I'm sure the kids are scared. My oldest son, Tito, as my brother, would protect his siblings. He then threw me on the bed where I was raped. I was just a rag doll and all I could think of was oh God, let this be quick."

I thought, what else can I do? When I tried reporting him, I was told that was not rape. He is your husband. Well, he was done and so was I. His last words to me: " when I get back, you better be here!!!!... If you are not, I will kill you !!!" He left and did not return that night. I cried all night. I could not take this anymore. I thought Maybe next time I won't be so lucky... Morning couldn't have come soon enough. I dressed the kids, and with not much of a plan except to just escape... I needed to run, but where could I go? With nothing but what we had on, I thought, I couldn't go to any family members, he would find me there. I figured I would go to the women's shelter.

Two months had passed, and somehow, he found out where we were and convinced me to go back to him, against all of the advice of social workers and therapists. I believed my abuser would change. That change never happened. I prayed the shelter would take us in. I couldn't afford to be on a waiting list. This was an emergency. I desperately needed their help. So, I grabbed my 3 children and walked down the hill of the countryside, in Puerto Rico. There was a bull in the middle of the street, literally. And of all the days I had my youngest child wearing a red t- shirt. I don't know if the bull story is true about the color red, but for me, today was not the day to find out. So, I had a side-chat with my oldest son, Tito " You're going to carry Erika, I'll carry Alex and we are going to run as fast as we can and we're not looking back. Oh my God help us!!!!

Well, we made it to the Shelter for Battered Women & Children Called "Casa Julia de Burgos. It was a Saturday morning, and the administration office was closed. Thank God, some of the girls were still there and remembered me so they let us in. After 6-months of being in the shelter with my children in 1983, I was represented by a pro Bono lawyer from the shelter's own attorney for my divorce. I will never forget that day the Judge said "I'm going to free you from your abuser, just pay the stamp ". I reached into my purse, nothing but 4 quarters to my name, which the judge gladly accepted.

Years later, I relocated to California as he continued to harass me and use the children against me, even in spite of living with another woman who was his lover while we were married. My grandmother, just as she did when I was a child, took care of my children and instilled the love of Christ in them, the same as she did with me.
In the early 90's the family was now in California. Internally I was a mess, and violent movies were something that triggered terrible memories in me that I thought had been buried for a long ago. The

trauma was deep and real. (I probably had PTSD).

Mother's Day 1998, My daughter Erika said she was going to church. I figured, why not it's Mother's Day so we can surprise mom and grandma'. It was the Best Mother's Day gift for them, the two lost sheep were going to church. I put my bottle of Captain Morgan, and my Newport cigarettes up. I'll see you guys later, let me gain some points here" so I thought. As I said before; when one's lost, I suppose it's good advice to stay where you are, until someone finds you. That day, I allowed Christ to find me and enter my heart, totally surrendering my life to Him. Both my daughter and I experienced a strong conviction during the sermon. At the end Pastor Ruiz gave the altar call tears were running down our faces uncontrollably. I cried out, ``I'm so sorry Lord, please forgive me" I felt waves of Living Waters, cleansing within me. That day He began to change my heart and showed me the Love I was missing from my father and husband. Through Jesus I've seen and felt the weight of unforgiveness, and the peace of liberation that forgiveness brings. I often thought of my dad, who has since passed, and my ex-husband living in Puerto Rico, I always thought I had forgiven them, I think it was more of "out of sight out of mind". But it wasn't, not for the Lord.

In July 2016, our annual convention "Church of God Assembly of Emanuel" was to take place in Puerto Rico. After 35- years I was able to visit the island again. Surprisingly enough my daughter wanted to go and visit her dad, and the woman that was his lover while we were married. I'm sure they had their reservations, and after some time I was invited inside their home too. We sat at the table, drank coffee, and laughed. There was no fear, hatred, resentment or even pain…

I shared Jesus Christ and the power of Forgiveness.
I've been given a new heart in Jesus Christ, and it is capable of loving and forgiving, and through Him, I've been Healed. You see Forgiveness is to extend grace to those that hurt you. I pray today you know that this is possible through Jesus Christ.
The Bible teaches that there are no lost causes. no permanent pit-dweller except those who refuse to leave. Every person can know the complete redemption of Jesus Christ.

Psalm 40:1-2
"I waited patiently for the Lord;
He turned to me and heard my cry.
He lifted me out of the slimy pit,
out of the mud and mire;
he set my feet on a rock
and a firm place to stand".

Throughout the years, every so often, my children will visit their dad and financially take care of his needs as his health has been somewhat delicate as he is a diabetic.

May 5th, 2022, a few days before Mother's Day, my Children received an alarming call from Puerto Rico. Their Dad had a stroke and so the next day they all hopped on a plane to Puerto Rico. I remember getting on my knees, crying, praying, Father I ask that you prepare his heart to accept you. I felt terrible for my children who, of course, have families of their own and now they would need to take on the responsibility of caring for their dad. Now this is where it gets interesting, I was praying and I asked (verbatim) " If needed, Lord, I will help the kids with their dad. `` What was I thinking? Well, "don't' ever doubt God, He does hear our prayers."

On June 14th, 2022, my children decided to bring dad to Las Vegas, Where he is loved, and cared for. Occasionally I sit with him, feed him as he's lost his vision and we reminisce about when we were young. I am reminded through Jesus Christ; I have been healed from unforgiveness to forgiveness in love. When I felt by the Holy Spirit move me to be part of this book, I never imagined that the Lord would have me share on Forgiveness. I can honestly share with tears in my eyes and peace in my heart, that I no longer see my abuser. I see a man that Jesus died for as he did for you and me. I have truly experienced forgiveness, and this feels good. I pray you come to a place of forgiveness through Yeshua Messiah.

Forgiveness Is……
"Bear with each other and forgive one another if any of you have a grievance against someone. Forgive as the Lord forgave you."
Colossians 3:13

†

BC Chaplain Estrellita Perry

Estrellita is a seasoned Bilingual professional Paralegal in the Immigration field, ESL Teacher, Transformational Life Coach, Bible Care Coach and an end-to-end Leaders shaper, a true encourager in any field. She is Certified First Responder from CERT and EVP (Emergency Volunteers Program from Israel), she got green belt in Karate and has performed in competitions at a national level in volleyball representing her country - Costa Rica- and in Fencing, for national College competitions. She owns Eagle Power, a Translations and Immigration Services company that dedicates time to help families around the world in their legal matters. She is also a Freelance Writer; actually having a column for the Metro PD Newsletter every month and excited for launching her first book in October 2022. Due to her integrity and transparency in her job, she has also worked for the Department of Homeland Security in very strategic special assignments, where she got many Certificates for her dedication and performance. She has worked for the Justice Court and now she works at the District Court of Nevada, where she assists Judges during Trials and performs complex tasks of high importance for this State. Her passion has been Volunteering in the community and she has done it through: BOSS (youth Christ centered ministry), Metro PD in Las Vegas, STAR Coalition against Pornography, HOME-TEAM Dallas- where she helped to feed 6000 homeless every year among other Christian singles, Celebrate Recovery- where she has mentored around 500 women, Friends of the Family- where she supported around 100 women from the Abused Women Support groups, RISE - where she functions as an Advocate against Human Trafficking, Hope for Prisoners - where she functions as a mentor, Juvenile Detention Center - where she ministered and CUMI (Covenant Unlimited Ministries International) where she has helped
She has been ordained as a Sr. Chaplain from the Chaplaincy Nevada; she is a Licensed Marriage Officiant, and she got certified as a Transformational Life Coach and Bible Care Coach, besides other titles. Her mission is her Ministry, which is based on Prophecy, Leadership, Discernment, Exhortation, Teaching, Intercession, Healing and Deliverance, which she has been exercising for over 15 years. She lives in Las Vegas, she enjoys her time with her son, hiking, swimming, loving life and pursuing excellence in everything she does.
Although she has obtained hundreds of Certificates, Awards and Recognitions; at the end, she always says people will never remember that, but they will certainly remember the Jesus who lives in us and use us to love on them.

† Forgiveness And Memoirs
By Estrellita Perry

I was born on April 9th many seasons ago in Costa Rica, but my mother's family was from Spain and my father's family was from Germany. I am a survivor of physical abuse, domestic violence, generational curses, abandonment, and anemia; among others, and saying that" I am a miracle and a living proof of the living God", would be the right statement to confess; and this is my story and journey to forgiveness.

I am the youngest of three. I have two older brothers - eleven years and twelve years older than me, so, growing up I never felt I had a family since my brothers were never at home, my father was absent most of the time, and my mother was not very talkative nor affectionate at all.

My oldest brother started using drugs and consuming alcohol since he was very young, and my other brother was never home because he was really angry at my dad. My mother became passive, submissive, and unaffectionate; almost invisible; and I survived just by not calling the attention of anybody at home and being a great student and behaving to the max. Otherwise, if my dad became angry towards me; he always used a thick leather belt he had in order to hit me in the legs and my back, leaving me without walking for a couple of days, bruises all over and a pain that was just unbearable.

When I was approximately seven years old, I was abused by my oldest brother, after he got drunk, and nobody was home; and he did it sometimes. It was the most horrific and disgusting experience I ever had, and I was so afraid to tell anybody. I kept this secret for a while. When I finally told my mother, she just said: "Do not tell your dad because he would kill him", so I remained silent for the most part of my life, living in fear.

I did not sleep well, I distrusted my own family, I felt lonely and lost my sense of protection and belonging was gone. My mother never talked to me about it, nor looked for any help for me. I found out years later that my mother did not want to have me because she suffered a lot with my dad's abuse, and she did not want to have more children; and for years, it felt like my mother hated me and the fact that she did not defend me in any way, made me hate her too.

Growing up was very scary in my home, because besides the fact of my abuse, we all suffered domestic violence from my father. He used to hit my mother often, my brothers used to fight against my dad to the point that blood came from their noses and faces, and the neighbors called the police to stop the chaos.
Hearing my father's steps in the house was terrifying; as we all expected the worst, mainly when he told us he would kill us one day,

which caused me to go to bed early, lock my door and keep my eyes open, until I got tired of expecting the worst to happen.

As I turned eight years old, me and my parents went to Mexico to visit some of their friends. This couple had three children, and the oldest was a very strange teenager girl who always was staring at me in a very evil way. It turned out, she had asked my parents if she could take me to her High School and show me around, and my parents approved it. She took me to a big mall in Mexico City after class, and she told me to sit on the bench and wait for her; but she never came back. Hours passed and it became dark. I remember I asked God to make me invisible, and I think He did, as nobody saw me nor talked to me for hours; until my parents came with the police to get me. I guess I was in shock; images of my family passed by like a movie in my head and I thought I would never see them again. I cried after we get back home, and my insomnia became worse. At that time, I had no idea what forgiveness was, and I hated my brother, I feared my father, and got angry towards this teenager. I experienced solitude, fear and anxiety and I could only cry on my pillow when everybody was asleep.

The same year: there was a cousin of mine who was two years older than myself who asked my parents if I could spend two days at her sister's house, and my parents agreed. So, she picked me up, we went to my cousins' house, and next day, she took me to a store. We walked there and she told me to sit in a box out of the store. I did that and waited, but she never came back. I was abandoned again, and I cried in silence with the hope that God would do something. Around two hours later, my oldest cousin and her husband came to pick me up and I was taken to my parent home immediately.

Hatred against my family increased and my level of confusion and distortion of reality too. I even remember I told God I didn't want to live like that anymore, but it is obvious He had other plans for me for sure. Meanwhile, I continued witnessing violence in my home, and I even witnessed my father raping my mother once in a very violent way. Those images were in my head, and I carried that trauma for years. I remember, my family never talked about offenses nor forgiveness; so, I grew up believing this was the way other families lived as well.

My childhood was characterized by fear, isolation, submission, and lack of trust; effects caused by events that terrorized me every day and every night as a child. I thought about my abuser, and I hated him for years, I even asked God for him to die, as his presence caused me re-living the abuse and I always felt uncomfortable with his presence. I did not know what to do with all this, and I felt desensitized for a while.

Then years passed by, and I found myself in college. During one of the parties, "a friend of mine" put something in my coke, and I did not remember anything until next day; when I woke up, I realized I was being abused. I was so angry, that I hated my life and I hated myself, and I thought for a long time it was my fault, and that maybe

I did something that caused it. But I knew a little about God at that time and I started reading the Bible every night; and that soothed my soul and gave me comfort. I was not sure what it was, but I started to feel safe when I had my Bible in my hands.

That was only the beginning; as the devil has tried to destroy my life in all ways (health, finances, jobs, relations, harassment, slander, lies, etc); but he has always failed, not because I am great, but because I am special to God, and He loves me that much. What God started in me through Jesus, my Savior, He will finish it with power. As the Bible says: *"The thief comes only to steal and kill and destroy; I have come that they may have life and have it to the full". John 10:10.* No one can beat the Creator of this Universe; and if I am still alive. breathing and smiling, the enemy has lost.

After that, my life turned in a roller coaster full of wrong decisions, bad companies, and awfully bad relationships. I became angry and ended up marrying the wrong men too. I got entangled in abuse circles and could not differentiate between healthy and unhealthy relations anymore. I remember when I was punched in my face and my eye became swollen and very purple, I thought I was going to lose my eye; and after that I continued in the same toxic relation for a time.

Years after, I moved to Texas. I married there after a while I found out my ex-husband was an alcoholic, a womanizer and used my skills to help him with the Business we had, which we lost after the divorce. After the third incident, when he used a knife trying to cut my neck, I knew my life was at risk and that I had to do something to change the course of it; not knowing at that time that I was pregnant. But the Lord gave me a certain assurance that I will be ok and my baby too. I filed for divorced and had to use a Special Protection Program to hide and be safe.

Then, I started to see a light at the end of the tunnel. I was rooted in a wonderful church where I made lots of good genuine spirit filled friends, and I was equipped in so many ways. I started to volunteer in the community and became a leader of the church for social, children, homeless, singles and youth projects.

A friend of mine talked to me about Celebrate Recovery, and I said: "Sure, why not? I do not have drinking or substance problem, but I will it a try. That was when I heard for the first time about the word "forgiveness" and how people have been set free. Although I had no idea how it worked, I made the decision to get into it because I wanted what others had, peace and freedom. When I finish this Program and after more than thirty years of my life; I could finally forgive the first person in my entire life; my abuser; and then, my mother. From that moment on, I felt my heart opened up and there was a sensation of clean air purifying my chest. I even talked to my abusers in person and told them that after all, I forgave them for everything they did to me, not knowing the motives, but without need to know it either. To the other ones, I forgave them before the Lord, and my past to be free was unlocked.

That was the point in my life where I started my journey of Forgiveness; not only to forgive others for the horrible things they did to me, but to forgive myself too. The insomnia continued for years, and I always checked my door was locked when I went to sleep every night. It has taken me years through Counseling, Deliverance sessions, Soul Ties Classes, Spiritual mentoring, and lots of prayer, in order to heal. I literally felt chains falling on my feet when the breakthrough took place and I felt something inside of me was made new. All those years of pain, abuse, tears, hurt, and shame were buried as soon as I forgave. What a wonderful breaker!

After that, I have become an advocate for the ones who do not have a voice and the ones who have one but do not know how to use it. I am thrilled how my testimonies have brought encouragement, healing, hope and empowerment to others; that is a way for us to be light in this world, and be an extension of Jesus on earth; at the end, like the Word says in *Matthew 11:5: "Whoever has ears, let them hear"*.
I am grateful for being alive, being healthy and being whole. It is funny how people see you and judge you for your exterior and the way you carry yourself; but they never know what we have been going through.

I have dedicated my life to my awesome son and to others; because I know I am a miracle; and I will make every second of my life count for the miracle God has made in me. As many of you, I am a survivor of many battles; and that is a strong indicator for me that my assignment and purpose in life are supernaturally orchestrated and diligently entrusted to me by my Father in Heaven.

Life is not about titles or degrees on the wall; it is about how clean and pure we keep our heart and our motives after our trials, struggles and tribulations; and how we use the teachings of our journey and apply the lessons to our lives, and share them with others. A heart full of "narcissism", "denial", "toxicity", "bitterness", "selfishness" and "unforgiveness" is a dead heat; nothing can be done, unless we deny ourselves and submit to the process of healing and reconciliation with and within ourselves.

Although I have gone through a lot; "casualties" of life do not determine who I am anymore, and they will never do. I always tell the people I mentor that "scars tell me where I am coming from, but they do not dictate where I am going to". I am learning throughout time that what is an inconvenience for some, or a time of adversity for many; it is becoming an opportunity for me; an opportunity to get closer to God, to hear His Voice, to understand the lessons of life; but mainly, to become a better version of me. Life gives me a chance to forgive no matter how painful the process would be; knowing that at the end, I will look back and say: "Thank you Jesus"; you were always with me from the beginning to the end; you were just watching me, proving my obedience, and testing my faith. At the end, when my time comes, I want to have a smile in my face and say: "Jesus, you were worth it every second of my life"; and finally,

I will see my faith being crowned; hearing the voice of my Father saying: "Well done, my faithful servant".

I know the Lord is the author and finisher of my story, and I know He is not done with me yet. I have learned that people will never remember our titles, awards, recognitions, or possessions; but they will certainly remember the Jesus in and within us. And that is why I am making sure that my life is worth living, worth telling, worth sharing, and now, worth being written.

I pray that my story will not only be one more you read, but the one you need to read in order for you to know that there is a God that loves you, sees you and cares for you. I pray that through my words you find encouragement and peace; knowing how important forgiving others and forgive ourselves is in our lives; because Forgiveness is the key you need to unlock and get your life back. Receive the gift of Forgiveness, embrace it, and use it. When your Forgiveness moment takes place in your life; you will contemplate a beautiful tapestry designed especially for you, where all your

Memoirs remain as a reminder of your journey. Remember that when God is with you, and you abide under His wings, all the darts thrown to you to destroy you, would always go straight to the cross. Thank you for reading my story and making it part of your flag for Victory, for His Kingdom.

Chaplain Della Frank

Della Frank is married to Anthony Frank and has three adult children, Simona, Nathan, and Jacob and three beautiful grandchildren, Mikayla, Sophia, and Vincent. Ms. Frank loves to read and hike.

Della is an ordained Chaplain for Messages of Faith Ministry (MOFM) and a commissioned worker by the International Network of Commissioned Workers and a small groups coach for the International Church of Las Vegas (ICLV). She is a member of the International Coalition against Human Trafficking. She is a leader in developing Human trafficking "Underlying Issues Trafficking Presentations" for Native American Tribes in Nevada. Ms. Frank presented at the 2022 Early Learning Institute Steering Committee on "Educating the American Indian/Alaska Native Student." She is a contributor to Empowerment Begins with Knowledge an MOFM Administration Department team member, and an Academy Instructor, and a member of the Academy Endorsing Body.

Della has provided workforce training to youth and has served the Native American community in various capacities, and she serves as vice-chair on the Nevada Indian Commission Advisory Board.

Della co-chairs the Education Working Group for the City of Las Vegas Mayor's Faith Initiative. She served on Governor Sandoval's Schoolwide Safety Task Force. Ms. Frank has a background in mine safety and was a licensed Emergency Medical Technician I and II, an Emergency Medical Services Instructor for Nye County, and a security officer authorized under the International Foundation for Protection Officers for the mining industry in central Nevada.

Della earned a Master of Education degree in Advanced Teaching and Leadership with an emphasis in Administration. Her undergraduate studies earned her a Bachelor of Arts in Secondary Education, with an emphasis in World Languages specializing in Spanish and a minor in Physical Education. Ms. Frank earned an Associate of Practical Theology Degree from Christ for the Nations. She holds additional Nevada endorsements in English Language Acquisition and Development and Technological Innovations.

† Forgiveness is My Legacy
by Della Frank

Luke 23:34: "Father, forgive them, for they do not know what they do."

I dedicate this story to abused and neglected children who, like me, were born to selfish moms and dads who did not parent them; and, despite all the chaos, have chosen forgiveness as their legacy. A web of dysfunction is the reality of many children enmeshed within "messed-up families." It is not easy to forgive parents who would rather entertain the demonic spirits of witchcraft named meth, heroin, or alcohol than spend quality time with their children. Or parents who prefer to embrace the demonic spirit of lust, which drives wounded parents into the arms of a stranger for a few temporary thrills. As a child, I ran away from my dysfunctional web and left to my demise, struggling to navigate through life and falling prey to Satan, the God of this world.

Unknowingly, I was in a war I was not prepared to fight; because of my ignorance, Satan had free rein to steal, kill, and destroy those entangled in our family web, including future generations
John 10:10.

Matthew West's song titled Family Tree addresses generational curses that, like a tornado, gain strength and intensity as it destroys one family after another. Generational curses can be passed from the things we hear, see, and experience and they can unleash demonic forces in one's life, leading to a vicious cycle of sin or addiction. The lyrics to this song skillfully convey to the listener how easily one can become mentally, emotionally, and spiritually bound up from dysfunction - or even possessed by demonic spirits. Family dysfunction is evil controlled by the spirit of ignorance, selfishness, unforgiveness, and rebellion. Demonic forces never hesitate to exploit times of havoc in a person's life, especially in children. The lyrics continue by asking the listener, "Are you going to be like your father was and his father was? Or are you going to be like your mother was and her mother was?" Will you be the one to stop the cycle of generational curses and make forgiveness your legacy? Forgiveness awakens the soul to break the power of generational curses.

My story begins by introducing my absent father and my disconnected mother, whom I will call Sam and Lucy. Sam was missing from my life physically, but he was not absent from my mind. I spent many nights obsessing over why Sam was not present. Sam was a rolling stone with a "free love" mentality, pollinating all the flowers he liked but beholden to none. Sam had 28 children and failed to provide praise, support, and unconditional love to any of them. He needed to develop confidence and high self-esteem in his children so they could become happy and 2 prosperous adults, however, he was too self-absorbed and indifferent to bother with providing any fatherly love.

Proverbs 13:22 a: "A good man leaves an inheritance to his children's children...."

What I inherited from Sam during my two encounters with him changed my life indefinitely. I was five years old when I accompanied my mother to the local bar, and Sam happened to be at the same bar. Lucy thought it was fitting to introduce Sam to his children. I had never seen Sam before, only heard about him. I remember the experience piercing my little heart with so much emotion and wondering what I had done to make Sam not want to be around me. I recall him reaching into his pocket, pulling out a quarter, and handing it to me. A feeling of insignificance flooded my being, and the spirits of abandonment, rejection, and rebellion were now my inherited reality.

My second encounter with Sam was when I was hitchhiking as a teenage runaway. My friend and I jumped into the pick-up truck of a man willing to take us to our destination. I started to make small talk about mining since my new stepfather was a high-level boss in the industry. I mentioned my stepfather's name, and Sam said he was once married to my stepfather's wife. I was a bit perplexed by what he said, so I had him clarify his statement. It finally dawned on me that Sam was talking about my mother, Lucy. I asked him for his name, and he identified himself as Sam. I revealed my identity, which made the circumstances uncomfortable, especially when he started reprimanding me for hitchhiking. Unfortunately, the conversation escalated to him bad-mouthing Lucy and her family for creating an environment that would cause a young teen to run away. Hearing someone else put down Lucy only made me defensive and protective of her, which was unfamiliar territory for me. Despite my relationship with Lucy, I stood up with courage to defend her honor. I said, "At least my mother stayed around to raise me. Where were you?"

The heated discussion eventually turned into dead silence until he dropped us off at my uncle's home never to be seen again. Sam never contacted me or sent me a birthday card. Sam does not know his grandchildren or care to know them. Nonetheless, I have chosen to forgive Sam for not being a dad or a grandfather. Millions of children are growing up without a father. Fathers matter and are essential to how children see God. When fathers are absent from their children's lives, they taint how their children view God the Father. Furthermore, children get their identity and security from their fathers, which affects a child's self-esteem and builds the foundation for how a child will relate to 3 others. Children are vulnerable to anything and everything this world offers without a strong identity. It is much easier to center your life around God and his presence when you have a loving father in the home to set an example for the children.

Absentee fathers are a problem in America. According to Focus on the Family, nearly 20 million American children —almost 1 in 4— live without a father in the home. Sadly, children in this situation face severe challenges. Statistically, they are more likely to grow up in poverty, drop out of school, and get involved in violent crime (Fatherhood, June 8, 2022). The following are statistics we cannot ignore:

- 71% of all high school dropouts come from homes with absent fathers.
- 85% of all youth in prison come from fatherless homes.
- 90% of all homeless and runaway children come from fatherless environments.
- 70% of teen suicides occur in homes where there isn't a dad.

Of equal importance, if not more, are mothers.

Many women, especially in some cultures, have very little decision-making power over their lives, as was the case for my mother, Lucy. She had an arranged marriage to a veteran at age 14 and gave birth to twin girls at age 15. She raised them independently after her soldier lost his battle with alcoholism. Things were difficult for Lucy as a single parent and only worsened when she met my father, Sam, who was also an alcoholic and a womanizer. Lucy ignored all the red flags and set no boundaries in her relationship with Sam. Without a marriage commitment, Lucy became pregnant with me and my younger sister; consequently, she now had four children to raise alone while trying to hold a job without a formal education. Lucy was always angry, and my sisters and I lived in fear of a short-tempered mother who irrationally grabbed the closest thing to her to discipline us, creating an unstable and dangerous environment for her children. Rebellion and anger were the generational curses Lucy unknowingly passed down to me.

According to the 2021 United States Census Bureau, 4 out of 10 children were born to unwed mothers. Single motherhood has grown so common in America that today 80% of single parent families are headed by single mothers - nearly a third live in poverty, and 52% have never been married. According to many Christian leaders, three things will almost assuredly keep women out of poverty: 1) get a job, 2) graduate high school, and 3) don't have kids before marriage. Many young women make decisions regarding relationships based on emotions and ignore any sound judgment. They tend to select a partner according to their potential rather than for their track record. Women must make wiser decisions about relationships for their children's emotional and spiritual well-being.

1 Peter 5:8: "Be sober, be vigilant; your adversary, the devil, walks about like a roaring lion, seeking whom he may devour."

Because my parents were not sober, they were unaware of how their selfish acts changed the trajectory of my life by opening doors to spirits that paralyzed me emotionally as a child and left a massive hole in my soul. The numbness I felt at age 11 made me vulnerable to drugs to relieve my internal pain. I not only had difficulty identifying my emotions, but I also struggled to navigate my feelings, especially the emotions of intimate relationships. Overwhelming fears of abandonment haunted me, leading me to abandon relationships prematurely, convincing myself that I was not good enough. I had no hope and forgiveness as my legacy was a far-fetched aspiration that seemed impossible to achieve due to the built-up anger and resentment that weighed me down.

I felt anger towards God for allowing me to be born. I was constantly blaming others for the lack in my life and for not having the tools to control the turmoil I was experiencing. Often, I wanted to yell from the rooftops, why did you have kids if you wanted to party all the time? In my young mind, my mother and my absentee father were the guilty culprits condemned for the crime of failing to provide a safe place to grow into a healthy, contributing individual. Lucy and Sam had other priorities of "greater importance," and it was painful to know that their priority was not to nurture their children into healthy, well-adjusted individuals.

Hosea 4:6a: "My people are destroyed for lack of knowledge."
Jeremiah 29:11: "For I know the plans I have for you," declares the LORD, "plans to prosper you and not to harm you, plans to give you hope and a future."

Although I have no recollection of being held or cherished as a child, God had a plan for my life, and he sent a Christian lady named

Madie, who introduced me to the lover of my soul who would never leave me or forsake me. It was not until Madie attempted to lead me into a sinner's prayer and a prayer of forgiveness that I realized how bitter and unforgiving I had become towards my family. While Madie started to pray, memories of hurt, lack, and anger flooded my mind. She told me I needed to forgive all who had harmed me, but I stopped her midway through the prayer and said, " I cannot do that! I cannot forgive them."

5 Matthew 6:14-15: "If you forgive others the wrongs, they have done to you, your father in heaven will also forgive you. 15 But if you do not forgive others, then your father will not forgive the wrongs you have done."

On a side note, I was reluctant to forgive the wrongs done to me; yet Jesus hung on the cross between two criminals at a place called Calvary, where they brutally crucified Him and the criminals, one on the right hand and the other on the left. According to the gospel of Luke, Jesus said about those who crucified him, "Father, forgive them, for they do not know what they do." Therefore, I could forgive those who hurt me. Madie insisted that forgiveness was my only option if I wanted God to forgive me for my sins. I finished reciting the sinner's prayer and verbalized by name those who had harmed me, including Sam and Lucy. Madie taught me two lessons that day, how to forgive and why to forgive. Unforgiveness almost kept me out of heaven and prevented me from having a personal relationship with Jesus Christ. Thank God that Maddie took the time to walk me through the process of forgiveness. God's love and grace broke through my hardened heart, removed the root of bitterness, and restored my relationship with my mother; forgiveness broke the power of generational curses over my life and her life. The negative feelings of depression, anxiety, abandonment, and hatred attached to me since childhood left me and was replaced with God's unconditional love. I was born again and set free from the chains that bound me. Everything in the world was beautiful, and God filled my heart with His love, which compels me to go into the highways and byways (the jails and the prisons) to change the course of generations.

In summary, God restores broken lives by taking an unforgiving heart and filling it with God's love; therefore, transforming one's legacy into one of forgiveness. No one has perfect parents; I get that. However, as Christians, we must not be ignorant about generational curses that keep many families in darkness, living daily with the four "Ds": depression, disappointment, discouragement, and defeat. Demonic forces are the only explanations for why a parent would choose not to care for their children. For children to have the best chance in life, two things must occur: 1) children need to have a mother and a father to balance development, 2) and children need to learn God's Word. Spiritual warfare is the key to breaking the chains of generational sin, but someone must be the warrior who will stand in the gap for the family to help break the chains of generational curses. Forgiving parents who do not create a loving and nurturing environment for their children is not easy. Those who have deeper wounds from their childhood will have to trust God to walk them through the process of forgiveness. My advice is to become an addict of the Word of God to renew the mind and find a Bible-believing church that will equip the family to do spiritual warfare against demonic attacks.

Proverbs 22:6 says, "Train up a child in the way he should go, and when he is old, he will not depart from it."

As the Matthew West song asks, "Are you going to be like your father was and his father was? Or are you going to be like your mother was and her mother was?" The choice is yours but remember your decision affects the children. Declare and decree that a dysfunctional family is not your legacy nor your destiny. Break the chains that bind you with the power of the Holy Spirit and choose forgiveness as your legacy; your reward is the abundant life Jesus promises us. I will be praying for you.

John 10:10b: "I came that they may have life and have it in abundance."

James 1:5: "If any of you lacks wisdom, let him ask of God, who gives to all liberally and without reproach, and will be given to him."

Isaiah 61:1-2a: 1 "The Spirit of the Lord GOD is upon me because the LORD has anointed me to preach good tidings to the poor; He has sent me to heal the brokenhearted, to proclaim liberty to the captives, And the opening of the prison to those who are bound. 2a to proclaim the acceptable year of the LORD...."

Babul, D. D., Luise, K., & amp; Luise, K. (2015). The fatherless daughter project: Understanding our losses and reclaiming our lives.

Avery. Fatherhood: How to be the dad your family needs. Focus on the Family. (2022, June 8).
Retrieved July 16, 2022, from
https://www.focusonthefamily.com/parenting/fatherhood-how-to-be-the-dad-your-family-needs/

Meyers, M. K. (2018, January 1). Fatherless daughters: How growing up without a dad affects women. We Have Kids. Retrieved July 15, 2022, from https://wehavekids.com/family relationships/When-Daddy-Dont-Love-Their-Daughters-What-Happens-to-Women-Whose-Fathers-Werent-There-for-Them#:~:text=Fatherless%20Daughters%20Have%20Self%2DEsteem%20Issues&text=Countless%20studies%20have%20shown%20that,her%20father%20isn' t%20there.

West, Matthew. "Family Tree." https://youtu.be/LlqH5-T9WtI.

SR Chaplain Shirley Ann Lyons

Dear Diary: Let me say a few words about me. I am the middle child of my parents, one sister and brother older, and two youngers. I remember very little about my childhood where I lived before the age of five. I just know we lived somewhere, with four walls and a roof. As I was told by my older sister, that I liked to get a pot a spoon from the kitchen and go outside and make mud pies.

Therefore, every summer when our parents were working, my younger sister and I would spend the days with our Big Mama at her apartment, one summer day while on a visit, my Big Mama's boyfriend liked to drink Budweiser Beer in the tall cans. He, ask me to place three cans in the freezer, not knowing there were three of us, and now we had our very own tall can of beer. Boy, it sure was good and cold, you have to remember this is Vegas and, in the summer, it gets 104 degrees or hotter.

As we finished our beer, my Big Mama noticed we were drunk from the beer. Big Mama was not happy with her boyfriend getting her grandkids drunk. Whereas, she had to call her daughter and explain what had happen, and then my mom was not happy. Therefore, my brother who was not much older than us was called to come and get us.

Shirley Lyons graduated as an ordained SR Chaplain on graduation day of, November 5th 2022.

† Forgiveness Is a Fork in The Road
Shirley Ann Lyons

Forgiveness is a noun. The action or process of forgiving or being forgiven. This word Forgiveness is not a word that is not in many people's vocabulary, especially when it comes to family. I came from a family of seven, three boys and four girls. Five of us grew up with our biological parents in Vegas, and my older brothers grew up with my grandparents my Mom's Dad in Texas.

What is the true meaning of Forgiveness?
In general forgiveness is a conscious, deliberate decision to release feeling of resentment or vengeance toward a person or group who has harmed you, regardless of whether they actually deserve your forgiveness.

There are three types of Forgiveness they are:
Exoneration – the action of officially absolving someone from blame.
Forbearance – patient self-control; restraint and tolerance.
Release – allow or enable to escape from confinement; set free
What is the meaning of Forgiveness in the Bible?

Forgiveness does not mean, forgetting. Rather forgiveness means letting go of the pain the incident is causing us. We forgive to give ourselves peace of mind, and in the hope that one day someone will return the favor if we ever offend them.

Why is Forgiveness so important to God?
We are made new; we have the promise of internal life with our Heavenly Father. Just as God forgives us of our sins and the many ways in which we wrong others. God commanded us to forgive one another. God did not only die for our sins, but also for the sins of those who have wronged us.

This is my story. I feel when we speak about forgiveness we must start with our parents. I'll start with my mom, remembering back on my childhood it was okay we always had our basic needs taken care of but nothing more. At an early age I never felt any love from my parents especially my mom. Dad always worked and mom was a stay-at-home mom, and dad worked nights so he slept during the day.

Daddy was a twenty-one dealer and a pit boss at the Sands Hotel and Casino. So, dad was the provider. Whenever I achieved something good in school I would go home and tell my parents about it, they're reaction was that's nice, never any fireworks, claps handshakes, hugs, or even showcasing it on the refrigerator door to show any pride in it.

I recall when my mom would wash and press my hair for church or school, there was one time I remember so vividly as if it was yesterday, getting my hair pressed my mom had the pressing comb so hot it felt like I had third degree burns in my head. I had tears running down my face and letting mom know it was burning me and the only reaction I received was as she had her hand on her personality (hips) was I'm almost done so be still.

When she was done, I remember running into the bathroom and immediately checked my scalp for burns or redness, then I put my head under the cool running water to relieve my burning scalp. Boy, my mom was mad as heck at what I had done especially after the work she put in on my hair. I didn't care at that time, so I had an afro until the next time. I got wise I would sit in the chair before mom came into the kitchen to do my hair, I turned down the stove to low hoping she wouldn't notice, and it worked.

I felt my mom hated me all the time, in the back of my mind I thought maybe my mom had an affair and secretly she was afraid I was not my dad's child. But I will never know.

One summer I was home, and my dad was napping, mom was cooking and needed some milk from the store. I walked to the store as I did many times without worry, and whatever the change was left I purchased a candy sucker. On my way home as I was walking I noticed a young boy on a bike kept circling me trying to hit me with his bike, so I walked a little faster I went through the open fence by the park I thought he was gone, but he was hiding behind a power grid.

He jumped out and grab me, put one hand around my neck and his other hand he tried to put in my pants, when I let out a scream, he punched me right in the mouth; then he let me go, grabbed my stuff and hopped on his bike and rode off with the bag of milk and my sucker. I ran home as fast as my legs would go. I opened the front door crying and running into my mom's arms I told her what had just happen.

The fireworks started. My dad woke up from my screaming and came running down the hallway, mom explained on what just happened. My dad put on his shoes and grabbed his .38 with extra bullets in his pocket, we exited the house with me walking behind him like it was the Wild West, and we did live on West Street.

We walked to park across the street from our house, and some teenage boys were playing basketball they looked up and saw a man with a gun, and girl with a bloody lip and an ice pack. Then my dad asked me the question? Is this him and my response was NO. I was praying to God very hard, hoping we didn't come across the boy on the bike. I was too afraid of losing my dad at an early age, going to jail fortunately for me we didn't find him. The teenagers felt sorry for me and said you're going to be alright, and I was. Now the summer was over it was time for school to start, all of the things which happened during the summer was now in the past. I had entered the fifth grade, and the last year of elementary school.

When I turned ten years old while I remembered my mom coming into the bedroom which I shared with my sisters and wished me a Happy Birthday, but it was not what I expected, closed fisted punches me on my butt, as hard as she could hit me, I was in tears mom had been drinking and it was early in the day. I cried and was screaming at the top of my lungs, hoping dad would hear me and come in and ask; what the hell, what are you doing to her, but it never happens when dad is at home. My sisters just look at me and they're eyes were as big as saucers. Once I got up and dressed for the day, my mom had a strange look about her but one I can't explain however it was almost like the devil. My day started and ended in pain.

As I got older this little girl was hoping for a least a hug or a kiss from my parents for any little thing, but that never materialized. So, I developed a passion for playing sport's that was my outlet for not being home. I was now headed to junior high school, we moved to a new neighborhood new friends and new school. I joined a softball team within our community; our team's name was the Foxy Ladies (I hated that name). It was an all-girls team. All of our games were mostly played at Doolittle Softball Field, which was within walking distance from home. I was hoping since I was playing softball within the neighborhood mom would attend some games, but not one, not even one. I was so hoping we could walk to the park, and even have a mother daughter conversation, which would have been nice.

Playing softball in the local area, I also participated in a variety of many activities at Doolittle Recreation Center. I recall being at the recreation center one afternoon on a Saturday hanging out with friends just enjoying the day, and I notice the boy who tried to harm me many years earlier we locked eyes, by now I was taller and bigger, even in my inner thoughts; try the same thing now, as you did years ago, and see what you'll get.

Our team was okay not the best, but I like the game of softball as the years went on, we got a little better, but not by much. I had a regular position, but I was also a utility player which means, I played where I was needed. Many years later I would meet Billy playing softball, Billy's team would practice before ours and he would stay and talk with our coach, as they knew each other.

Coming home from practices or games, dad would need a shirt for work to be pressed and I would be the one home to complete this task, mom would be passed out on the couch from drinking and my dad would be so frustrated with mom, but he had to go to work. After mom would sober up and dad competed his shift at work, daddy would wake us up when he came home and threatened to divorce at least two to three times a week; mom would sober up say she's sorry and dad would forgive her and unfortunately, I would be hoping that this was it, but it never happened.

When I was a sophomore in school and a cheerleader, mom had a massive heart attack and spent the whole Christmas break in the hospital, I was afraid I would lose my mom. Mom didn't get discharged until the next year, so mom was hospitalized for a total of three weeks. This was a wakeup call for our family as a whole, mom stopped drinking and smoking. Life as I knew it was normal for me. But as she had gotten better, though mom's attitude towards me didn't change. The day I met Billy my mom officially hated him, but my dad on the other hand adored him, daddy had another man he could talk cars talk with.

As time went on and I gotten older, graduated from high school got a job and moved out. Living with my mom had gotten to be worse and more than I could stand, even though my dad didn't want me to move out at such a young age. I explained to my dad one of us has to go, that's your wife even if she is mom I'm moving out. And I never looked back. Later my mom became my (BFF). When I would get off from work, I would even stop by on my way home for a short visit and ask her how she was doing, but one thing I knew I had my own place to call home. When I told my mom I was expecting a baby her response was as usual negative towards me and say Billy doesn't want you or that baby why would you want a baby with him.

On March 27, 1983, Billy and I welcomed a baby boy named Demetrius Allen Scott.

As time went on, I was able to purchase my first home, unfortunately daddy never had a chance to visit, my dad passed shortly after I moved in, November of 1994. But in spirit dad saw it. When mom and my sister came up for a visit and they arrived, it was when they actually entered my home, I was so proud of myself and the accomplishment I achieved, and to my surprised mom said to me, I proud of you kid, this gave me so much joy in my heart.

During my mom's later years, she developed Dementia. So, mom would come and spend the weekends with me and weekdays with my other siblings, after we found mom a permanent place to live, I went to visit her at least three time a week. Whenever mom needed personal items, I was the one they phoned, but I was okay with it. I guess what I'm saying is, there was a time that I needed her forgiveness, but I know she loved me the only way she knew how. I forgave mom of the past, but I'll never forget it.

When I told mom that Billy had passed, and by her having Dementia she didn't remember him or chose not to. I'll never know.
Whereas Billy and I never married but our union lasted for thirty-five years. Unfortunately, Billy passed on June, 18, 2014 at the young age of fifty-years and eight days. Demetrius was so heartbroken of the passing of his father and so was I. Mom passed in

May of 2017, I never felt sad or uneasy about mom's passing; I guess because I kept
in contact always. I stayed in the room with mom until Palms came. I held her hand and told her I'll stay until they arrive, the other family members waited outside. The hardest part for me was when they zipped up the bag, I knew it was all over.

The day we buried my mom, the grandsons were the pallbearers. I bowled in a tournament at the Texas Station I was calm and relaxed the whole day, no one knew I laid mom to rest. To this day they still don't know. Even in death Dad is still with Mom, they are buried side-by-side.

In conclusion: As it is written Ephesians 4:31-32
Get rid of all bitterness, rage and anger, brawling and slander, along with every form of malice. Be kind to another, tenderhearted, forgiving one another, as God in Christ for gave you.

☦

Chaplain Mike Puccio

Mike lives in Las Vegas
Mike is from Downey California.
Mikes wife is Rachel, and their sons are Michael and Caleb.
His grandchildren are Claudia, Penelopie, and Michael.
Mike graduated from the University of Redlands Kingsmen Drum & Bugle Corps
He was employed by Pacific Telephone, but he is now retired
Mike served in the U.S. Army for 11yrs
Mike served 35yrs in the Royal Rangers as a Chaplain, Area Commander, Training Chief
His Frontier/Pen Name is Ropeholder

Mike has been an ordained Chaplain since May 2021.
He serves on the RECAP Team assisting law enforcement call-outs for homicides.

† Are You Strong Enough to Forgive
By Mike Puccio

Many people find it hard to forgive those who seek to go out of their way to hurt others. Telling someone it was okay when they have wronged you seems like asking them to repeat themselves. When they see no consequences for their actions, they may even justify their behavior, and I, having been greatly hurt, was one of those. Looking back on a painful past, I had to ask my mother why there were such heavy feelings about my dad. She told me I was too young to remember because I had just turned three and that my father had beaten my brother and me for messing up his new car. If I were three, my brother would have been eighteen months old.

We had just gone to the market, and my dad remembered something he had forgotten. My mother and father left us in the car while they went back into the market. All those groceries on the back seat floor were too much for us not to explore. My brother found the eggs and smashed them on the rear seat and windows. I busied myself by digging into the box of Rice Krispies for the toy surprise. I could only remember that much of what happened. What followed, I have no memories. My mother said it was horrible, and my dad went into a rage, hitting us and then whipping us both. My mother said my brother had welts under his diaper; she thought about leaving my dad. I believe God was merciful to me by not letting me remember, only a need to keep my distance from him. Under this oppression, I would never be good enough. I would try to have him like me, but it was easier for him to show rejection. He said I wouldn't live to be fifteen.

As I grew, the not knowing why things had become the way they were, I became bitter. Still, one must learn to forgive. As important as it was for Jesus to include forgiveness in His prayer. *Matthew 6:14, "For if you forgive men their trespasses, your heavenly Father will also forgive you."* So, what is forgiveness? It is an act of kindness from the heart. It could be said that forgiveness is better than sacrifice. *Matthew 18:35, "So likewise shall my heavenly Father do also unto you, if you from your hearts forgive not everyone his brothers their trespasses."* God will not forgive us unless we forgive. Be ready to forgive and prepare yourself. The Apostle In his letter to Timothy, Paul wrote that he should *study to show his approval. 2Timothy 2:15.*

We must be ready not to fall apart when we are harmed. Remember the words in the Sunday School song, "Be bold, be strong, for the Lord our God is with thee." When we only feel our pain, we fail to see the hurt in others. What would have caused our dad to want to harm us? Was there a tremendous spiritual battle inside him? Like so many others, in losing this battle, did he turn his anger on that one he could hurt the most? A kind word turns away wrath. In my approach, I tried to be slow to anger and soft, as in Proverbs 15:18. I was twenty-one when my dad took that for weakness and said," You are not tough enough to be a Marine; I'll sign you up for the Army. "I did not want to be the source of contention. I thought I would listen and humble myself as before God. And if then what I may hear is true, the first person I must forgive is me. I would not excuse myself for wrongdoing. My surroundings, the time I was living in, and those around me may have influenced me. But I alone am responsible for who I am because I have chosen this lifestyle. I found that forgiving yourself; you are the hardest one you will have to forgive. All the "I should have" and "I shouldn't have" memories that kept bringing me down just saved me from living a victorious life.

I began to pick myself up, shake it off, and make myself a better person. Holding a grudge is a terrible waste of energy. It was keeping me run down and too tired for me to do anything else. I separated myself for a while, reading my Bible, nine chapters a day. To start, three chapters in Genesis, three chapters in Matthew, and three chapters in The Book of Acts cross-referencing every verse. When I wasn't reading, I was praying. One afternoon, I felt so depressed and alone sitting on my couch. Suddenly I felt someone put their hand on my shoulder. My back was to the wall, so how could that be happening? I looked over my right shoulder and caught a glimpse of a man standing behind me. I fell to the floor. I thought I should be afraid, but you cannot be afraid in the presence of the

Lord. I rolled over, and He was gone.

I have always had faith in God, and now I know I'll never be alone. God gives freely, and freely we receive; the choice is ours to make. Read John 3:16 if you want to know what God is like. He never asks us for something He doesn't make way for us to accomplish. What is the source of my strength? If you ask anything in His name, He will do it. He said nothing should be impossible to those who believe. One must believe that God can do anything. I made peace with God. Look around, and see all the wonderful things, He has made. The heavyweight that we carry is sometimes more than we can bear. We give our troubles to Jesus, don't blame Him. He who was willing to die for us will be our friend like no other. God's love is all around us, but if we would only love Him, He will fill our hearts with gladness. We will become new people. Our old ways will become distant, just a thing of the past. Having asked for Jesus to come into our hearts, we will feel so clean. Not like if someone was to touch us that we would become somehow dirty, but that in touching others, they would become clean. Sharing this feeling is contagious, spreading from person to person because everyone wants to be clean.

God is always ready to forgive; as a loving God, it is His nature. Has our need to pray been overshadowed by our past? Do we believe our prayers should not be answered because of all of the bad things we have done? Have I decided that if I can't forgive myself, how can I expect God to be willing to forgive me? I'll look at myself; remember the Old Testament prophet *Isaiah 43: 25-26. wrote*, "God *declares that He will blot out your transgressions for His own sake and will not remember your sins."* This is so like God to want to forgive and to forget. We do ourselves harm when we do not ask for forgiveness. Our God is also known as the way maker, the God that forgives. So, if we have been forgiven, in some ways, when we pray, in bringing up our past, we bring back to God our old nature, that He is not holding against us. We 'remind' Him of things He doesn't want to remember. He only knows that we are forgiven and if I remind Him, then haven't we placed a roadblock in His way? Remember, God wants to forgive and forget to clear the way. This kind of open line of communication is what Adam had in the garden, the same as Jesus had while on earth. It is the same, with no difference, from what we can expect to have now.

To know God, we must try to understand Him. The Bible says, "God is love." People in love want to be loved, show their love, and express it before others, like a lighthouse on a hill, a light that cannot be hidden. God waits to forgive and to love. The Bible, in *Isaiah 45:23, also says that every knee shall bow and every tongue shall confess,* and in *Matthew 5:5, Jesus said, "The meek shall inherit the earth."* Understand meekness is not a weakness. It is tough to stand alone. It takes courage, and a mindset like David wrote in~
Psalms 1, "He shall be like a tree planted by the river, that shall not be moved."

Where do we gain this kind of strength? We all have faith, but do we use it? Do we exercise our faith to have confidence in God? On a visit to my local gym, I looked at what was happening inside. I notice the people working behind the counter; don't they look healthy? Now look at the personal trainers; don't they look buff? Think about all they had to go through to gain that look. That probably didn't happen overnight. No, they had to work at it, they had to stay with it, and they could not ever give up on the hope that one day they too would become that perfect athlete they knew they could become.

Ask any of them how long they have been working out, and they will exaggerate their answer. It will a lot depend on how far out of shape they were. Some may even say they started and stopped several times before dedicating themselves to the long, challenging task in front of them. Forgiveness is like a good workout; one will decide to forgive and then change their mind. Remember, forgiving and not excusing myself comes first. If we are forgiven, it becomes much easier to forgive others. That is because, having found favor with God, we have His grace. Make peace with God, and then He will direct our path.

Grace is unmerited favor. That's right, we do not deserve it, we cannot earn it, but we must accept it. It is freely given, you must freely receive, and that is through faith and believing in Jesus Christ. *I Peter 3:15 says we are to be ready to provide an account of the hope in us.* It is only by God's grace that He sent His son Jesus. If I only think of myself as someone who can't be forgiven, then I don't understand God. He can do anything; in fact, nothing is impossible with God.

How often have we turned away from God's resources to try our skills, only to be turned away in weakness? Sadly, and with the best of intentions, our best efforts do little more than get in the way. We look for doors to open in front of us when the knob is in our hands. *Revelation 3:20, Jesus tells us that He is standing at the door knocking.* But that we must open the door for Him. He wants to forgive us, but we must first ask Him for forgiveness. A blind man once heard that Jesus was coming up the road. *Luke 18:35-43. He cried out to Him, "Jesus have mercy on me." The people in front of Jesus told him to hold his peace. But the blind man cried louder, "Jesus of Nazareth, have mercy on me."* When people get ahead of God, they often make mistakes. Again, they told him to be still. The blind man yelled at the top of his voice, "Jesus, thou Son of David, have mercy on me." Jesus noticed him and motioned for him. The people said, "Well, He's waiting for you." The blind man got up and went to Jesus. Then, Jesus asked him, "What would you have Me do for you?" "That I may have my sight,'" he answered.

It may seem that it should be evident to us what a blind man would ask from Him. But Jesus knows our every need and all of our heart's desires. Maybe it was something other than his sight that the blind man wanted most. There are many other unseen good reasons to call out to God. It was healing for someone else, salvation for a family member, or even forgiveness for things done long ago. Jesus wanted him to ask. In healing him, *Jesus said, "Thy faith has made you whole."*

What we are waiting for may never come because the one that wronged us is still only seeing their hurts. Sometimes I think that Jesus healed the blind only so that the crowd could see His love and forgiveness clearly. Like the angels told the disciples in *Acts 1:10, "Why are you standing around gazing upward into heaven?"* Jesus had just given them the great commission. As He was telling them what He wanted them to do, Jesus did not mean sometime in the future; He meant for them to go now. You wait on the Lord only after you have submitted your request. So too, forgiveness should be asked for and given now. Don't just wait around idly looking for the next thing to come.

It has been said, "That is the scope of things eternal; this is not even a moment." We waste more time than necessary when we wait for the other party to say I am sorry. In the fourth chapter of his book, *James wrote, "Life is but a vapor, that appears for a little time, and then vanishes away."* So then, we need to get up and forgive those who have abused us. Don't wait because life is too short. Don't wait because someone will miss out on receiving healing; it might just be us. At the end of that chapter, *James wrote, "When you know the right thing to do and do it not, to him it is a sin."*

People will make mistakes, but to forgive them is what Christ wants. He, from the cross, made way for us to be able to do so many more things than we would have believed possible. *Luke 23:34, Jesus speaks, "Father, forgive them for they know not what they do."* Jesus forgave those who had called for His death and the soldiers who crucified Him, even as He died. He forgave them because He could see that they didn't realize what they were doing. We must forgive those who have harmed us, or the mistake will be ours.

In our daily lives, we miss things; we don't see or hear them; we don't even notice them, do we? It is like us to believe that we are going unnoticed; because of this, we will do things and think no one was hurt. But the little things we do that "won't make a difference" add to a lifestyle of offenses. Jesus told about a man traveling from Jerusalem, Luke chapter ten, that was beaten and robbed by thieves. He was left to die by the side of the road. Then by chance, a priest came, and he crossed over to the other side of the road, thus avoiding the man. But then another man came and stepped over him and continued on his way. Thinking, as the man was already hurt, why not avoid, or ignore him?

However, in forgiveness, executing a final solution over a quick fix may be more than some can bare. The scope of the problem usually grows with indifference. We have probably heard someone say, " It's not my job," "That's not my responsibility," and "Why should I be the one?" So, if it's not our job, is it everyone else's? If we are not responsible, should someone else be appointed? It's not, "Why should I be the one" but when will we be that one? Again, don't wait; take care of the problem. Don't let it continue becoming so overwhelming, ask for and obtain complete forgiveness.

When Good Samaritan saw a man that he did not know but saw a need, he was moved to compassion and took care of the traveler. He did an act of kindness from the heart because he had business else ware. Fortunately, some are willing not to be unforgiving. Whether by experience or the drawing of the Holy Spirit, like the good Samaritan, do that which is right, forgive, and take responsibility for making things better like they can be. A good Samaritan would rather face trouble once than avoid it twice.

After several attempts through the years to make amends with my father, this past January, my dad came down with COVID. At ninety-two, he decided not to take the vaccine. He left no will, saying it would be someone else's problem when he was gone. Stubborn almost to the last, he called me from his hospital bed. He said," Michael, I love you; I am going to heaven." This was his way of forgiving me and asking for forgiveness. An hour later, I received a call telling me my father had died.

Throughout our daily routines, a sense of uneasiness waits. It is a fear of not being up to the task in front of us. Fear comes from someone else's assessment of our ability, probably based on prior performance. And not wishing to be overwhelmed by this feeling of uncertainty can lead to terrible decision-making. To overcome this fear, we must take an inventory of our lives and determine our place in life. God has never failed us yet. When asked, He has always forgiven us. He has promised that He will always hear our prayers. Man is our brother, and as God is our father, Jesus said that we should be known for our love for one another. To know love is to give love. We all need to be loved, as God is love, so greet one another with love. Be ready to forgive.

†

Chaplain Susan Clark

Born 1948 in Imperial Valley, California. Her father was raised a farmer. His parents lived in separate houses. This emotional and physical separation carried through into the immediate family. They did not know how to love nor forgive.
Susan, a high school, college graduate with bachelor's degree in Education majoring in English Literature and minor in Physical Education. She has a Registered Nursing license. Two major life occurrences were
her motivation. One was the care of her mother who had a degenerating genetic condition called Huntington's Chorea. Body movements become constant. Activities of daily living require help. The other was caring for her husband Greg, comatose for three years. Then he died. Greg fell eight feet striking his head onto concrete becoming comatose.
Through the above experiences, Susan, at sixty years old, learned the importance of life. Christ is life. She moved to Las Vegas better opportunity existed. One difficult day, church ladies presented a sign, "Free Prayer Here". Susan pulled over. They sang, "Jesus loves me this I know, for the Bible tells me so."
Susan knew this from long ago church school. Her family was not Christian. She attended church Sunday. A greeter prayed over her. Susan asked Jesus into her heart. The following week she attended Holy Spirit
Conference. A Pastor prayed over her; she went down. Tears poured; she was "slain in the spirit". She forgave all those who had hurt her including herself and continues forgiving all. She now sees people with different eyes. Jesus forgave us when we were killing him on the cross. He asked the father "forgive them for they know not what they do". He asks of us 'This is my commandment that you love one another as I have loved you" John 15:12.
At sixty years old, she learned the purpose of life "follow Jesus. Jesus is love, forgiveness and eternal life,
he died on the cross to reconcile us to himself. She was set free.

† Forgiveness is Truly Loving Another
By Susan Clark

Relationships will all eventually require true forgiveness. Forgiveness is a healthy act. What is true forgiveness? Jesus Christ is a significant example of true forgiveness. Jesus Christ, the only son of God, creator of all, came willingly to this earth. Virgin Mary birthed him. He came from heaven to become flesh on this earth. Jesus was crucified on the cross willingly. Christ shed his blood over us, enabling Father God to look upon us and not see sin. Jesus arose three days later, overcoming death, hell, and the grave. Jesus Christ lives eternally!

Those who accept Jesus Christ as the son of God, Savior, and Messiah will also live forever. Jesus died to give us eternal life. While dying on the cross, he said, *"Father forgive them for they know not what they do, and they parted his raiment and cast lots."* Luke23:24.

Jesus requested Father God's forgiveness for the Roman soldiers who crucified him by nailing him to the cross. They pierced his side with a spear. Jesus loves us, as is shown by forgiving the soldiers who virginity. I thought I would feel some love. The opposite occurred; I felt guilty and increased loneliness. We broke up yet. We continued our friendship. My oldest sister, Sondra (not her real name), attended college. Sondra had become like my mother and had obtained a teacher's license. She married Jonathan (not his real name), the college president's son. Both esteemed themselves intellectually. They invited me to spend one summer with them in California, and I did. One night both Sondra and Jonathan began discussing lifestyles with me. They asked me what I thought about multiple couples. I replied I had not experienced nor thought about that situation.

Both Jonathan and my sister defended it intellectually. They said they believed it to be morally permissible if all participants agreed. Jonathan stated that he believed that shared sexual experiences were a way of knowing one another. My sister agreed with him! I was inexperienced, nor had I ever thought about sharing sexual experiences. Now I had lost another mother. I was mourning inside.

I returned home. I was currently a senior. Greg and I began to date again. We did date others, which made me feel confused regarding the way I was living or dating multiple boys. I did think about what Jonathan believed. Greg graduated in 1965 and obtained a full-time job at Holly Sugar Corporation in Imperial Valley, a factory that processed sugar beets into sugar. The factory closed in the summer for repairs by the full-time staff.

I graduated from high school in 1966. Greg and I reunited; we lived together in his grandmother's house. His grandmother told us to get married if we continued to live together in her house. We complied. We became a married couple. The situation looked good on the outside. But there were arguments on the inside. Greg would drink, becoming very intoxicated and staying out late. He would come home late without calling me, especially on Friday nights. There were times we would sleep separately.

One afternoon there was a knock on the door, and there stood Skipper. (not his real name) He was known in our school for his preference for the same sex. I felt my heart stab again as he inquired if Greg was home. I answered. Again, I felt completely alone. My own family never visited. Greg returned home. I approached him with the topic of what did Skipper want. My heart was pounding. Greg asked me, "What do you think?" I asked, "You"? He said, "Yes." His defense reminded me of Jonathan's and Sondra's conversation. He stated that we are all humans with varying likes and dislikes. If the participating parties enjoy one another, he does not see an issue or care about the marriage vows.

I was confused by not knowing Jesus, true love, forgiveness, or what sin is. I was left out, invisible, crushed again! I was pouring emotional tears. Greg did not try to comfort me in any way. What he did do was "party" that night. He worked the next day, hungover. It was summer, the season for full-timers to do factory repairs. Greg was full time. There was a protocol for the second floor, it was to lower the broken piece through a removed floor grating hole down to the floor below. The men repaired the fractured piece on the floor, which was safer. The nut from the equipment piece required loosening, and Greg should have applied a lubricant for 30 minutes. However, Greg was impatient since he was a weightlifter capable of pushing 300 pounds. He loosened the nut manually, and the nut gave way suddenly. Greg fell through the gaping hole. He hit his head on the grate, knocking himself unconscious. He fell eight feet to the concrete floor below, hitting his head again.

I received a call at approximately eight p.m. It was the hospital! My husband Greg, whom I did love, had been admitted to the Intensive Care Unit (ICU), regardless of what he disclosed to me. His eyes were currently open. He was striking out at us, attempting to get out of bed. I was traumatized and in tears. I was also intermittently angry with Greg. He willingly drank. He probably would not have fallen if he had maintained sobriety.

Afterward, Greg went in a coma with eyes closed and intubated; therefore, the doctors contacted a neurosurgeon from Arizona. The next day the surgeon Dr. Strong (not his real name), arrived. He immediately transported Greg to the operating room. The word of his condition was out, and relatives and friends lined the hall waiting for the report. When Dr. Strong entered the hospital hall, all was quiet. Dr. Strong reported that the right brain was highly edematous.

He had inserted a shunt draining the collected serous fluid from the swollen brain to the body's systemic drainage. The shunt relieves pressure off the nerves. Dr. Strong explained that Greg might open his eyes, but he's not out of the forest yet. He has a long way to go. I sat down on the floor, almost fainting. Greg's best friend, Thomas (not his real name), went down next to me. We supported one another.

Greg did open his eyes, yet there was no eye contact. He was extubated. He was fed with a peg tube and remained in a coma. His mother's pastor Ken (not his real name), spoke to me regarding faith. I did not know Jesus, Holy Spirit, or Father God. I had very minimal experience in prayer, what belief is, and what true love is. I angrily answered, "Show me where to get it, buy it, and I'll be first in line." Shortly following this experience, I went into the church while empty, and I collapsed onto the floor, weeping with my broken heart. This act was the closest attempt I came to any: faith, belief, love, and forgiveness that might begin to exist in me. I shut it down. I had zero experience with real love, faith, trust in Jesus, Holy Spirit, and the Father God. I did not know, nor have any idea, who they were.

In Imperial Valley, Imperial California, I completed my college requirements for secondary school teaching. I received my bachelor's degree from San Diego State College in Calexico, California. I majored in English Literature with a Physical Education minor. Greg was transferred from the acute care hospital to a Long-

Term Care facility. Then He was transferred to a Long-Term Care Rehab Facility in Fullerton, California. He was transported via air ambulance; I rode with him.

Greg died on his birthday, October 26; he lived four years in a coma. He was approximately 25 years old; he died on the day he was born. This date touched my heart. The funeral was in Imperial California. I returned to Fullerton, California. My passion was in Home Health Care. However, I taught two years of school: one year of junior high and one year of high school. But I was drawn to nursing due to my experience with Greg in the medical world. I returned to school and became a licensed registered nurse. This journey occurred in the '60s & '70s: Woodstock, free love, sex, drugs, and rock and roll. Satan was very active. just as he is today. Yes, I was a definite participant! I met my second husband in a high-class Laguna Beach bar.

Windsor (not his real name) had a very successful computer business. Windsor was an intellectual but did not know true love or wisdom. Windsor, unsurprisingly, was unfaithful. We divorced the second and final time. With this divorce, I felt no anger, no pain. I was numb. I wished him no harm. His first wife, Marianne (not real name), had one child Michael (not real name) lived on the same block. Marianne, Michael, and I became a little family bonded by our experience with Windsor. We shared a true feeling of loyalty, camaraderie, and trust in one another. We shared meals, helped with the cleanup, and watched TV together. When one had a need, the other would help. We had peace within one another. Michael was a joy. I wondered if this was what Pastor Dan was referring to when he spoke of faith.

The Home Health Care company I worked for moved to Nevada. They invited me to go, and I followed. I felt this would be a new beginning. I drove past the International Church of Las Vegas on one difficult nursing day. Ladies were standing in the parking lot holding signs saying, "Free Prayers Here!" That caught my attention!! I stopped. They prayed for me and then sang, "Jesus Loves Me; this I know, for the Bible tells me so." I recalled this song from the church school I attended as a nine-year-old. The message touched my heart deeply then and now. The following Sunday, I went to church, and a member named Janet Grady ushered me to my seat. Janet sat with me and escorted me to the altar post-service, where I asked Jesus into my heart.

The Holy Spirit Conference occurred the following week, and again, Janet and I went forward to the altar. I went "down" onto the floor when Pastor Pasqual prayed over me. I was "slain in the spirit," and tears poured from my eyes. I forgave: my parents, my sister, her husband, Greg, Winsor, and all those I know who hurt me. I forgave myself and continue doing so, forgiving all. I now see people with different eyes. Jesus forgave us when on the cross when we were killing Him. He asked the father, "Forgive them, for they know not what they do." He asked, "*This is my commandment that you love one another; as I have loved you" John 15:12.*

At sixty years old, I learned the purpose of life is to follow Jesus. Jesus is love, forgiveness, and eternal life. He died on the cross to reconcile us to himself. We are to follow Jesus in the great commission lovingly. Jesus said, *"All authority in heaven and earth has been given to me, therefore, go and make disciples of all nations, baptizing them in the name of the Father and the Son and the Holy Spirit, teaching them to obey everything I have commanded you. And surely, I am with you always, even unto the end of the age". Matthew 28: 16-20.*

†

Chaplain Joann Hamilton

Joann Hamilton, Lives with her husband of 54 years, and her older sister in Las Vegas NV. They have lived in Vegas since November of 2009. She enjoys visiting different states and of course seeing her children and grandchildren when they can match up schedules with them.
They became members of The International Church of Las Vegas in 2010. She served as a part of the new visitors connect team calling group that year through now. She has been a part of the women's table leaders, overseeing 3 tables, and facilitates with her husband small groups in her home once a week in the Fall and Winter seasons.
May 14, 2022, she became an Ordained Chaplain with MOFM of Nevada. She is still taking more classes to become better equipped for serving Jesus and ministering to people.
She has 3 grown daughters, Geneva, Grace, and Elizabeth, 5 grandchildren, who they get to visit as often as possible. She worked at Trinity Christian School Spring Valley, CA. in an after-school program called Power-Line Tutoring- in reading, comprehension, spelling, and math. When the funds ran out, she was asked to stay on and become a classroom aide and help the students in classroom.
Joann enjoys reading both for studying and for enjoyment. Two books, she read for enrichment and inspiration were REES HOWELLS INTERCESSOR BY NORMAN GRUBB and THE SERVANT: A Simple Story about the True Essence of Leadership by JAMES C. HUNTER. Both helped her to see how Intercessory prayer and Faith in today's world, can truly move mountains and help people with their everyday life.

† Forgiveness is Love
By Joann Hamilton

Hi, my name is Joann, a sinner saved by God's love and grace. I was between 4 and 5 when I first asked Jesus to come into my heart and ask him to forgive me for my sins. Grandma Hope led me in the prayer of salvation. God forgave me that day; I know He did because, He has led me on this path of learning about His love, Forgiveness, mercy, Grace, and Faith.

When I was sixteen in our church youth group, we went to a Christian youth camp in Julian California. The camp speaker's name was Pastor Decker, he told us everything Jesus went through to pay for our sins, and he was pretty detailed about it. He explained how Jesus went through beatings, whippings, and humiliation for us; then He died on the cross to pay for all our sins. My friends, Lynn, Jean, and Sue and I were crying, that night because of all Jesus had done for us: We chose to make a complete surrender to our Savior Jesus. Love is an action and forgiving or asking for forgiveness, for me it is showing God's Love as a disciple and follower, of Jesus, my Savior and Lord. This is an important part of my walk with Him.

John 3:16 'For God so Loved the world that He gave His only begotten Son, that whosoever believeth in him should not perish but have everlasting life."

I just pray others will see that forgiveness is for everyone and God's Love is at the center of forgiveness! God never runs out of forgiveness or Love. Because of God's Love: Jesus gave forgiveness on the cross; yet Jesus's sacrifice for our sins has to be recognized and received by confessing our sins, and believing, and accepting Jesus's beaten body and shed blood was sacrificed for us and our salvation. Because we believed and received, God forgives us, and we will not perish but have everlasting life.

Luke 23:39-43 39 "Then one of the criminals who were hanged blasphemed Him, saying, "If You are the Christ, save Yourself and us." 40 But the other, answering, rebuked him, saying, "Do you not even fear God, seeing you are under the same condemnation? 41 And we indeed justly, for we receive the due reward of our deeds; but this Man has done nothing wrong." 42 Then he said to Jesus, "Lord, remember me when You come into Your kingdom." 43 And Jesus said to him, "Assuredly, I say to you, today you will be with Me in Paradise." 43 (NKJV)

The prisoner on the cross acknowledged that he was on the cross for his breaking the Law, and that Jesus did nothing to deserve dying for. This thief then turned to Jesus and said "Lord," remember me when You enter into Your Kingdom. This is where he believed who Jesus is and that He was the son of God and his savior. He had acknowledged his sins and believed in Jesus. He then joined

Jesus in Paradise that day!

This is what I pray that others will see in this chapter and all the rest of this book that we are writing.

John 3:16 'For God so Loved the world that He gave His only begotten Son, that whosoever believeth in him should not perish but have everlasting life." (NKJV)

When I ask for forgiveness from others, do I approach them with a Christ like attitude, am I humble and truly repentant when I ask the person to forgive me, do I do it with love, or am I asking because it is an obligation? I know there are times I did not ask for forgiveness with a fully repentant heart. Later I would go back because the Holy Spirit prompted me and showed me His grace and mercy to help me go humbly, in true repentance. Only then was I able to go back with His love and seek forgiveness from the one I offended.

Forgiving is love in action, to forgive, sometimes seems hard, but seeking God's heart makes it possible. He helps me to see the other person through His eyes. He knows their heart well. I cannot see their heart, but God can, so I need to listen to Holy Spirit's guiding me to those I need to go to and ask forgiveness from them.

I had gone to, my best friend Sarah, I had known her since I was ten. I would go to her house to play, and she would come to ours. We liked many of the same things, such as skating, reading, the same type of books. This was one of the things we would share and discuss was the books we read. I said something about one of the Horse stories she read, and we argued about it. Then she got upset about a comment I made, (which I realized was stupid now) it hurt her, and she left quickly. I never meant to hurt my friend. I really felt bad. I felt nervous about asking her for forgiveness, but I knew God loves us both. I wanted to ask for forgiveness from her and I wanted her to know I was sorry for what I said, and I really should not have talked that way to her. Repenting of my actions and words was hard, but I ask with love in my heart for her to forgive me and she said yes. Then both Sarah and I slowly rebuilt our relationship with each other and became good friends again.

When I was in my early fifties, my mother passed away the Wednesday after Easter; she had been sick with the flu and the cough would not go away. She did not have a fever, but she had trouble breathing and because she had COPD, we tried to get her to the doctor's office on Easter Sunday, she said no, but she promised to go on Monday when my sister could take her. So, she went into urgent care Monday afternoon, and they immediately admitted her into the Hospital.

Tuesday morning, I went up to her room and they had her on oxygen and breathing treatments. Her doctor said she had Pneumonia, he thought they could get it cleared up and she could go home by late Wednesday afternoon. Earlier that morning I went to the cafeteria and picked up things mom had asked for and nurses said they were ok for her. When I came back her Pastor, Reverend Wesley was visiting her, her comment was she wanted to make sure that everything was right between her in Jesus. I told her that was great, and that the doctor had said she would be going home Wednesday. We were all looking forward to mom coming home. On that Wednesday afternoon, my mother, Erma Lorraine Foster Stout, did go home to her heavenly Father and to see Dad again. We were expecting it not to end that way, but God has an appointment for each of us.

The next day my daughter gave me a journal my mom had given her to get an idea of how my mom and aunt grew up. There were gaps in it, but toward the end of the journal my mom had written several hurtful and untrue words about why she thought our girls had left home or went to work and moved out when they went to college. Most of these things mentioned were normal for young adults to do; her comments were that Larry, (my husband) and I were too strict and had to many rules. Others were things she said the girls told her. Regardless, because I could not talk to her, I could not let her know how she had hurt me and how the girls, and Larry and I had already asked forgiveness of each other and had forgiven each other and been reconciled.

Now that she was gone how could I talk to her and give my forgiveness for the things she thought of me and become reconciled in my heart. Years later I went to counseling and my counselor and her intern and I did role play and they helped me walk through it, by one of them playing my mom's part and I was myself. The counselor with the help of mom's journal played mom well. It was a long and teary-eyed session. I came out feeling in my heart that I had become reconciled to my mom, I had forgiven my mom. I felt at peace in my heart and soul. I still miss my mother; I know I will see her with Jesus in Heaven. Jesus also taught us that we are to forgive someone many times in the same day, if they come saying they repent, then we should forgive them.

Luke 17:4 "And if he sins against you seven times and seven times in a day, and returns to you, saying, I repent; you shall forgive him." (KJV)

Matthew 18:21-22 "Then Peter came to Him and said, 'Lord how often shall my brother sin against me, and I forgive him? Up to seven times?" Jesus said to him, "I do not say to you, up to seven times, but up to seventy times seven." (NKJV)

The scriptures above show that no matter how often a brother or sister sins against you if he or she comes with a repentant heart, you are to forgive him or her, each time. This is how forgiveness is, with God's Love in your heart.

Corinthians 13:4-6 Love suffers long and is kind; love does not envy; love does not parade itself, is not puffed up; does not behave rudely, does not seek its own, is not provoked, thinks no evil. Does not rejoice in iniquity but rejoices in the Truth.

When you look at 1Corinthians 13:4- 6, Love suffers long and is kind; love does not envy; love does not parade itself, is not puffed up; does not behave rudely, does not seek its own, is not provoked, thinks no evil. Does not rejoice in iniquity but rejoices in the Truth.

When I sin, I know I can go to Father God and tell Him what he already knows, but I go to God to confess and be forgiven and cleansed from sin and get my heart clean before Him. "Why" you ask? Because I love Him, and He loves me and is merciful and kind. It may seem to be a simplistic answer, yet it is the Truth.

While watching the news two or three weeks ago the story was about a man that had killed a small boy and did not seem to care in court. Then I thought something about him that he should be put away for a long, long time or be shot! I wanted Justice for the young boy and his family. Holy Spirit put a catch in my spirit, I had to go in a quiet place and ask Father to forgive me for that thought. God knows this man who killed this boy, only God himself knows what this man is called to do, I do not; God is the Just and merciful Judge; I love and trust God even if I do not understand Him.

Paul the Apostle was a murderer and pursued and tortured many of the new believers, but then Jesus, got a hold of Paul and he became a pillar of the church and wrote thirteen books of the New Testament. He believed repented and God used him to turn the world upside down.

John 1:9 If we confess our sins, He is faithful and just to forgive us our sins and cleanse us from all unrighteousness. (NKJV)

Our God Loves and Forgives because he sees us as cleansed through the shed blood of Jesus. Yet, when we sin, we still need to keep our hearts pure before Him Because He loves us, and we love Him we need to repent and confess our sin to Jesus. This way we can grow closer to His heart.

Matthew 5: 22-24: 22. "But I say to you that whoever is angry with his brother without a cause shall be in danger of the judgement. And whoever says to his brother, 'Raca!' shall be in danger of the council. But whoever says, 'You fool!' shall be in danger of the hell fire. 23.Therefore if you bring your gift to the altar, and there remember that your brother has something against you, 24. leave your gift there before the altar, and go your way. First, be reconciled to your brother, then come and offer your gift." (NKJV)

Reconciled; means to make amends to a person to seek a rebuilding of a past relationship, this in my mind is a part of forgiveness and being forgiven. Your gift that you left at the altar is not acceptable until you have made it right with your brother or sister. Now is the time to be repentant and humble; ask the Holy Spirit to help us to go in love and restore the relationship that had been broken, then give your gift to God, at the altar.

1Peter 4:7-8, "But the end of things is at hand; therefore, be serious and watchful in your prayers. And all things have fervent love for one another, for Love will cover a multitude of sins." (NKJV)

We need to walk in love and unity, learning to repent and forgive as soon as we can, so that no root bitterness or unkind thought, can cause us to sin and start speaking in a way that is speaking evil of anyone! This is giving the devil a foothold, and if you continue, he will be leading you the way you do not want to go.

Ephesians 4:31- 32, 5:1-2 31 "Let all bitterness, wrath, anger, clamor, and evil speaking be put away from you, with all malice. 32And be kind to one another, tenderhearted, forgiving one another, even as God in Christ forgave you."

"1Therefore, be imitators of God as dear children. 2And walk in Love, as Christ also has loved us and given Himself for us, an offering, and a sacrifice to God for a sweet-smelling aroma." (NKJV)

Even in the Old Testament we see forgiveness, just as Jesus was willing to die for our sins Moses says to God in *Exodus 32:32 "Yet now if You will forgive their sin—but if not, I pray blot me out of Your book which You have written." (NKJV)*

He said this right after the Children of Israel had made an idol while they were waiting for Moses to come off the mountain of God, where Moses had just received the Ten Commandments, God was extremely angry with the Israelites. Moses pled for God not to destroy them but forgive them, and blot his name out instead of the

Israelites, from God's book!

Mark 11:25-26 25. "And whenever you stand praying, if you have anything against anyone, forgive him, that your Father in heaven may also forgive you your trespasses. 26. But if you do not forgive, neither will your Father in heaven forgive your trespasses."

My prayer time and quiet time with Jesus; is very personal! There are times, He has brought to mind someone I need to forgive before I can get closer in my Prayer time with Him. He helps me to recall exactly when and for what it was I need to forgive that person. Then I will tell Jesus I forgive that person, and I will let them know. I have forgiven them for the offense or hurt. How I approach them and say it has to be in meekness and in love, because they may not know they hurt or offended me. You see I love God and people, so if Jesus says He will answer me then He will help me do what is right. Yet, at times I have failed to say it well. I still try to become reconciled with the person that I have already forgiven.

I have found that as I walk through the reconciliation process of forgiveness, it is not quick, because it involves two people and God is in it with us guiding us. It takes time, love, and patience to work through the hurt and offense on either side of the Forgiveness solution. Prayer, tears and seeking God's guidance will help. It can mean a sacrifice on my part so; the other person will see that I am really repentant in seeking their forgiveness. Both parties have to be willing to sacrifice to become reconciled, to each other; sacrifice time, pride, self-righteousness, and the hurt, so each person involved can receive, and be reconciled.

When reconciliation finally happens, it is so beautiful and the love for each other and God flows freely. At least for me it did.
If we look to Love and Forgive like Jesus does, we will start being more like Him in our actions and behavior. All the stories I gave have been through the people I am involved with and are my friends. Some people did not like me at first but came to know I cared about them and if I ask them to forgive me, they knew I truly meant it.

Offenses and hurts and lies come, but God's Love is greater than these. He will help me walk through them and He will help you also. Just trust and believe He will help you to Forgive and Love even your enemies.
Luke 6:27-28 "But I say to you who hear: Love your enemies, do good to those who hate you, bless those who curse you, and pray for those who spitefully use you."

Forgiveness opens the door to later being able to share Jesus with friends and enemies alike. Be ready for God to lead you through these open doors to be His Love, Light and Salt to others. Then be ready to let His Love and light shine through you!

☦

Chaplain Randall Patterson

Born and raised in Denver, CO, Randall has had a long-standing career onstage singing, dancing, and acting in Las Vegas and abroad. He's also called home to NYC, Branson, MO and Tokyo Japan among other places.

From lead singer in the iconic shows "City Lights" and 'Jubilee' on the Vegas Strip, and various musical theater shows around the country, to Headlining his own one man show, and touring with a Four Seasons tribute show, Randall feels blessed having been able to visit 75 different countries. Other attributes include songwriter, artist, (Randallscreations.com) and producing, directing, and choreographing his own 50's and 60's show. In finally following God's calling to be a chaplain;

"There is nothing like the thrill of being onstage, but nothing I've done before is as important, meaningful, or gratifying than sharing God's truth and love in helping hurting people. God has a plan – for each of us!"

† Forgiveness Is… Selflessness
By Randall Patterson

"To be a Christian means to forgive the inexcusable because God has forgiven the inexcusable in you."
— C.S. Lewis

When I picture forgiveness, I see our Savior Jesus Christ hanging on the cross. The supreme act of love, which took complete selflessness in sacrificing Himself to forgive us our sin debt.
Two things I have learned in life,
1. Forgiveness is paramount in order to live peacefully within yourself.
2. Forgiveness is most often over-looked, and underrated.
Meaning people too often ignore forgiveness and how it affects our mind, soul, and body. Jesus said in *Matthew 6:14-15* *"For if you forgive men their trespasses, your heavenly Father will also forgive you. But if you do not forgive men their trespasses, neither will your Father forgive yours."*

An unforgiving heart can block blessings from the Lord and emotionally weigh us down. From childhood trauma to adulthood heartaches, forgiveness had to take place in my heart in order for me to heal. Forgiveness was the key to my peace of mind.

Here is my story:

The Issues...
We unknowingly become victims of our circumstances when we are young. Broken marriages are prevalent today, but in the 1960's when my folks divorced it was very unusual. Growing up that way I really didn't notice it until instances such as going to the little league football banquet with mom because dad was 'busy' - That was embarrassing.

My father divorced my mom when I was two years old. We saw him every Sunday after church, into the evening until I was nine, then it became every other weekend. Those weekends were fun, but dad not being there on a daily basis was when he was needed the most. As a teenager, I felt let down a number of times by him and I was always seeking his love and approval. My oldest brother took the brunt of dad's bad temper with ruthless spankings. Dad could be very intimidating, and his harsh voice froze me scared as a child.

At one point as a teen, mom and I weren't getting along, and I wanted to move in with dad. He told me it was better that I stay with mom. The rejection I felt caused resentment and more anger. I eventually realized that he did love me, the best way he knew how. But the scars of rejection remained for years.

'Fathers, do not provoke your children to wrath; instead, bring them up in the discipline and instruction of the Lord.' - Ephesians 4:6
'Fathers, do not provoke your children, so they won't become discouraged.' - Colossians 3:21

Depression...

A number of things from a very early age affected me causing a struggle with bouts of depression including as mentioned above; not having a dad present on a daily basis, because there are times when a kid really needs a dad, or at least a good masculine role model to converse with and teach him things. And my poor mother, raising three boys basically on her own, being overly strict and overbearing trying to make up for it, really couldn't take the place of dad.

Mom having a very low income and being too proud to go on welfare, was a saint. She gave every bit of her heart in all her efforts, she always volunteered and helped everyone. That was her biggest love language: The gift of service to others. Everyone loved and thought the world of her. When she died over 150 people came to her funeral service to pay respect to this 89-year-old woman. I have nothing but love and admiration for her and the trials she had to go thru. Therefore, I hesitated to reveal some of this, but I believe there is an important lesson to be learned for all in this story - my story.

Being a single mom, working full time 5 days a week, without any prospect of hopeful future romantic life while stuck every day in the basement of the church as secretary, she would end up taking her stress out on us three boys - a lot. Mom was a hard worker, born on a farm she had that farm hand mentality, and if we weren't working or keeping busy to what she felt we should be doing, her words meant for encouragement (and also out of fear that we would go down a wrong path) actually became sharp jabs that ended up being detrimental.

It wasn't her fault; she was doing the best she knew how.
Years later I could analyze it and see her intent was for good, it's just that her method wasn't. But of course, I couldn't see that at the time. Her words stuck in my adolescent mind and convinced me that I was "lazy and good for nothing" and I "would never amount to anything" because of it. It did not make me strive to do better, it made me feel I was less than, and deserved to be - that I would never be good enough. Years later when certain things wouldn't work out my way, those words would still haunt me, and I would feel I didn't get to win that prize or excel at the project at hand, or get the job because I deserved not to. If only I could've understood her plight at the time, and grasped onto and understood what King David wrote in *Psalm 139:13-15* '*...For You formed my inmost being; You knit me together in my mother's womb. I praise You, for I am fearfully and wonderfully made. Marvelous are Your works, and I know this very well. My frame was not hidden from You when I was made in secret, when I was woven together in the depths of the earth....*
I was special and very important to God - we all are.

Feeling unloved…

When I was thirteen, it seemed like mom was always angry with me. I was confused by contradictory words and actions; she would yell at me for something one minute, turn around to tell me how much she loved me the next, the mixed emotions made me not trust that she really loved me. My thought process was since my brothers were four and five years older and mom wasn't always yelling at them, that maybe I was not really part of the family …Maybe I was adopted …Maybe dad left because of me? After a while of feeling unwanted and that I couldn't do anything right, one Friday night after dinner I'd had enough. Mom yelled at me for some reason, I grabbed my jacket and stormed out the back door - I ran away.

Obviously, I hadn't thought this out well enough because it was late October, and I only had a light army surplus jacket on. Didn't know where else to go, so I walked the 3 miles to our church. We had a large bus ministry and across the street from the church they were parked in an empty lot. I decided I would live on one of the buses, and live off the land, (even though we lived in the city)! As the evening wore on, I got hungry. And as the sun went down it kept getting colder! I finally realized I wouldn't be able to survive this way, but hatched a plan to teach mom a lesson, I would wait out the night, and then go home. I tried sleeping, but that didn't work, the seats were too small to lay down in and I was cold. After what seemed like an eternity, I decided I had punished mom enough, surely, she must be distraught, sitting there wringing her hands!

It sure was getting colder ...and I lay curled up thinking the sun would probably be coming up soon. I decided it was time to go back home. It just so happened my brother had left his bike chained up behind the church so I unlocked it and rode home as quick as I could. The conversations going thru my head seem comical now ...'mom must be worried sick, up all night drowning in her tears! Maybe she didn't really love me though... but hopefully she would fling her arms around me and tell me she missed me!'

As I took off for home figuring since it was so late, I would take the major streets home rather than the back streets but wondered why there was so much traffic out so early in the morning?! I peddled faster. When I got home, I was puzzled my brothers car was gone, I wondered if they must be out looking for me? The lights in the kitchen were on and when I walked thru the back door ...there was mom, in the kitchen, cooking something. She stopped what she was doing, turned towards me and instead of running to me with open arms she just stood there glaring at me with an icy stare. But wait! ...where was the anguish, the tears, the hugs? And what could she possibly be cooking so early in the morning? Then I looked past her to notice the clock on the wall; it was only 9:40 pm! I had only been gone about 3.5 hours!

Mom was mad when she sternly asked, "Where have you been?!" When I finally told her that I thought I she didn't love me, the look on her face softened, and it touched her to the core. She came over,

put her arms around me and told me how much she did love me. But I was stiff, still not trusting. It took a little while.
Incidentally, years later mom would apologize over and over for being so hard on us - (I never let her know how some of her words affected me, it would've made her feel bad, and some things are better left unsaid).

What friends…?

We were raised in a strict religious upbringing with a lot of legalisms. Everything was wrong it seemed. We couldn't go to movies, dance, or listen to rock music. We were told we couldn't be a part of the world or hang out with kids who didn't believe as we did.
- *Do not be conformed to the world, but be transformed by the renewing of your mind - Romans 12:2*
I have given them your word, and the world has hated them because they are not of the world, just as I am not of the world. John 17:14

Imagine my frustration and confusion when 'friend day' came around at church; "invite all your friends from school" the youth leader would say. The response in my mind was 'I have no friends at school because you've told me I can't, because they don't come to our church and don't believe as we do.' Sometimes it was very lonely and frustrating.

Now life wasn't all doom and gloom, we had fun and laughs, and some wonderful memories as other families have. But often times we are unaware of personal struggles our neighbors or even close friends face. Often, we can hide our deepest hurts and cover them up, so the world doesn't see. We didn't have school counselors to go talk to and depression wasn't something anyone really recognized or spoke of openly back then. In elementary school I was very shy and afraid of life. I think back on the kids that bullied me. How cruel they could be, and how insignificant I felt being too weak and scared to fight back. Or my little league baseball and football coach. All he cared about was winning, not about how he made a young kid feel. There is a certain type of cruelty by those who are in authority, and how they treat kids rather than 'coaching' them and teaching them how to play.

The Final Straw...

My past failures and depression finally came to a head when I was 42 years old. I could not figure out what was wrong with me. Why I felt so overwhelmed, down, lost. Why couldn't I make a relationship work?! Why did I still feel so much anger about certain things in my past?!Changes were happening in my life with relationship, work, and moving. I had read enough information about depression to know I had to root out from my past what hurt me, so I could deal with it. As I was doing so, as a Christmas present for my family I began writing some humorous short stories of my life growing up. But while I tried writing down a pretty funny story of me playing little league baseball, remembering the feelings of how that coach made me feel, he was downright cruel in his callousness. Honestly, to him he probably never gave it a second thought - but to me, how he made me feel after I made a major foul play when I could've scored a tying run where we may have won the game - wrecked my world! (And reinforced that conditioning that I'm a failure and deserve to feel this way).

For 3 days every time I tried finishing that story the tears would flow down my face to where I couldn't even see. I even thought 'why would I ever want to bring a kid into this world to end up a mess like me?' Pushing my psyche down into a black hole, felt like I was in a whirlpool spinning around and sinking deeper and deeper. That is when I finally cried out to the Lord. I appealed for help in Jesus' name. And what the Holy Spirit put into my mind and laid on my heart is 'You must FORGIVE HIM. Forgive ALL of them. Quit being selfish in your holding on to anger, what good has it done for you? Let - it - go!'

The astonishing story of Corrie Ten Boom came to mind. Forgiving the two men who caused her whole family to suffer and die in a Nazi concentration camp. "Forgiveness is an act of the will, and the will can function regardless of the temperature of the heart." – Corrie Ten Boom.

And the great example by my own cousin Wendy as she forgave the man, who raped and killed her daughter. She realized she could become bitter and allow it to eat away at her for the rest of her life or she could choose to forgive, and live. 'Lacy's Law' is now nationwide because of her. "Forgiveness is the fragrance that the violet sheds on the heel that has crushed it." — Mark Twain

My cousin's example is the fragrance of the flower of forgiveness. Jesus on the cross asked God the Father to forgive the men who were crucifying Him, mocking Him, having no sympathy in their cruel torture and killing. So how could I not forgive others who have done so much less to me?! It was at that point I fell on my knees praying, I verbally mentioned every person in every instance that I could think of where I had been hurt. And forgave them not just with lip service, but from my heart. I then asked forgiveness of the Lord for any and every hurt I had put others thru over the years. I then asked the Lord to forgive me of any unknown sin and hurt in my life. And finally, I forgave myself for too high of expectations, and for not putting the Lord first and living thru faith.

The most amazing thing happened to me while praying, I felt the heaviness, as if a weight was slowly lifting off my shoulders, becoming less and less. The imagery in my mind's eye was like being lifted out of that black hole. I could see light and it was becoming brighter. And when I finished that prayer, expressing thankfulness for what God was doing, and about to do in my life in Jesus mighty name - I felt a joy that only comes from the Lord. I actually - felt - lighter. Everything in my room at that moment even looked brighter.

I finished that Baseball story, and without adding all the emotional turmoil that affected me privately, turned it into a very funny story that I am happy to say my family laughed out loud at.
In offering true forgiveness we must be as selfless as Christ was on the cross.

✝

Chaplain Laura Bjork

Laura is a grateful believer in Jesus Christ who has led her to a life of redemption and salvation. Laura is recovered from drug and alcohol abuse and has been clean and sober since 2005.

She owns several businesses with her husband of 17 years. Laura operates a non-profit homeless outreach and serves more than 200 people a month called "His Works".

We are all His Work in progress through Him and extend our help through each other.

Laura developed an Empowering Women a speaker recovery meeting that is held once a week, for a local ministry called Spiritual Care Chaplaincy Program which is close to her heart, while sharing what God has done for her and for her recovery.

✝ Forgiveness, The Day My Eyes Really Opened
by Chaplain Laurie Bjork

"Come to me, all you who are weary and burdened, and I will give you rest. Take my yoke upon you and learn from me, for I am gentle and humble in heart, and you will find rest for your souls. For my yoke is easy, and my burden is light." Matthew 11:28-30

Since I was a kid, I have been unable to visualize everything or anything right in front of me. It was all a blur, and it got blurrier as I got older; even my kid, my spouse, and my home, everything was like a distorted image of what it was supposed to be. I felt like I was walking in an empty skin suit and unable to see, which is how I learned how to survive my feelings. The feelings of despair and emptiness fueled my existence resulting in "the blur."

Growing up I didn't know how to cope with feelings. My father, in didn't let us feel anything until he told us how to feel. I was angry about this; I wanted to feel and explore my feelings and thoughts, but I was trained not to. I grew up in New Jersey, where my life was decent. From the outside, it looked good. It looked like we had everything, but it wasn't like that; inside it was torture, all of the abuses I went through in one single home. I thoroughly thought that it was expected; little I knew at that time, it was completely dysfunctional. I felt like I never really fit in with them and something was off. Did other kids feel abandoned by their own families while living with them in the same home? I did not know, but I often wondered how it was for other kids my age.

My mother was Jewish, and my father was Episcopal; we celebrated both holidays, but neither parent had a real connection to either religion. They started sending me away to be with my grandparents in New York City, and I felt different there; I felt real. I felt like I could laugh, love, smile, and play, and I remember that in New York, my grandparents loved me; I could breathe and be me, and I felt safe.

Back home, my neighborhood was small and full of older boys. There was only one other girl my age, and she and I had become close while trying to survive the crazy older boys. They hated me, and I felt like it was the same miserable existence everywhere I went. They would give me such a hard time throwing rocks at my head and calling me all sorts of racial names; I just sunk into my feelings and thought, this is how I'm always going to feel. At the same time, I went to elementary school, where I felt even worse; I hated school. I didn't get good grades, I rebelled against everything and everybody, and I didn't have any friends.

The blur of loneliness even lingered there too. I always had meltdowns and would hide for hours upon hours curled up in a ball in a closet or a small area in the basement or the woods; it was quiet there, and my thoughts could rest, I was alone, and I was protected. I remember always being alone, and I liked it; it was my comfort zone, safe spot, and coping skills. Sometimes, when I was out of the house, I could laugh and do that freely, but I don't remember laughing at all in my house; it was like it was not allowed.

My parents were both in education, and I felt like they made me feel like a failure and stupid because I didn't understand school and embarrassed them. I got diagnosed with a learning disability and attention deficit disorder (ADD) and put on meds for that reason; that made my life even worse now, having to go to special classes and be an outcast even more. During one of our science classes, we were doing a DNA project, and my parents and I didn't match up; this is how I discovered I was adopted. My parents acted weird when I came home with this knowledge like I was wrong to discover that I was not biologically theirs. But then it all made sense why I felt like I didn't belong, and it added more feelings to "the blur."

The abuse got worse as I got older, and in my mind, I could understand more of what was going on and hated my life. The neighbor girl Mackenzie and I became close friends and would always talk about our future and how we could not wait to get out of that town; we were always outside and away from my home; and her home became a safe spot where she protected me, for which I spent lots of time there.

I started drinking at the age of 11, and this made me feel free and alive. The drinking increased, and my behavior worsened; I started breaking into neighbors' homes for alcohol and cigarettes. When I stopped the abuse at home, stuff went rough, more control, more mental abuse, and I felt lower than dirt, and I kept stuffing my feelings into "the blur." I acted out a lot in hypersexuality, which increased with both men and women; sex made me feel alive, and I got attention.

I was labeled a "run-away"; I was never at home and never at school. For this reason, my "parents" sent me away to a boarding school for learning-disabled kids. This place was not good at all; many out-of-control kids were forced to live together; this was a bad mixture of trouble. And the blur got worse there. I stopped going to school and found better things to do, like house parties, smoking pot, sex parties, and drinking. The drugs and sex got worse, and I remember I wanted to die because nothing would ever get better. I felt this was how my life would be forever, and I just labeled myself a depressed addict.

I learned early on that if I blamed my parents for how I was acting, it lessened my guilt and shame and made me a victim, but only to where I would get more attention. The more drugs and alcohol I used, the more my victim mentality took hold. There I felt better. It wasn't my fault that I was an out-of-control addict.

After school, I left and just couch-surfed around the east coast, making people feel sorry for me and using drugs and alcohol more and more; now doing things I never thought I would do for drugs, such as sex acts for a place to stay. I had no clue who or what I was anymore; the name I used was a "street name," and it was the only name I knew after forgetting my real name. I was that empty shell; all I felt was anger. I just put those feelings deep in the "the blur" and did what I had to do.

My relationships with others were also terrible and abusive, but physical abuse was the most common resulting in bad beatings. I wanted to run but did not know where. So, I had a great idea to move to Las Vegas, where I would be shipped off to and spend my summers with my family who lived there. Soon after I arrived, I realized that all my problems and feelings came with me. I found myself in more abusive relationships to feed my drug and alcohol problems. My spirit was gone. Where was God? Did He ever exist? I know that for a long time, I was asking myself how God can do this to people. But He did not do anything to me, I did it to myself, and He was waiting for me.

I used to go for treatment to get out of some cases I caught up in. In Vegas, the disease and the blur got worse, and I went into treatment, but I was never really clean and sober. I had many head injuries, waking up in hospitals not knowing what happened; I had many sexual assaults, a broken nose, and a face that required intense surgery, and I still don't know how it happened. My life was out of control. I tried to work but couldn't hold a job; my alcoholism and drugs were my life.

In my late 20's, I was convinced this was all I deserved. I experienced the same things from childhood to adulthood: anger, manipulation, and a lot of control. The overdoses, and alcohol poisoning didn't stop me; I wanted more chaos and found it. The abusive relationships I was involved in escalated to the point where someone almost took my life, and that relationship scared me. It left me feeling angry and lonely but mostly terrified. I feel like I had been kicked in the chest from fear.

I was on a dreadful run for weeks; I didn't show up to my job, so that was gone, this time the feeling of despair was the worst I ever felt, and I remember I was yelling outside for God to take me now and to give me a heart attack every time I hit the crack pipe. I was a mess crying in a ball, and my hair was falling out. I could barely walk; I wanted all this life to stop. I couldn't even tell you what made me call rehabs to get into a place, and I have no idea, and I couldn't remember anyway. I got to rehab, and they wanted to put me on so much med stuff just to get off the stuff I was already using, and I said no. I told them I wanted the stuff so I wouldn't seize.

The Detox process was weird, I felt my legs for the first time in years, and so many feelings flooded my brain. I asked God: Why did you save me? I kept asking why I am still alive. Then one day, I was sitting outside saying this, and a warmth came over me, and I felt alive for the first time in years; I knew at that time that God had saved me so I could tell others my story.

This was when I started believing that there may be a higher purpose for all this madness, so I left rehab and stayed clean. It has been a crazy journey, but now I am really living. I met a man, and I jumped into a relationship. I got pregnant during my first year in recovery; I had a good life, a boyfriend, and a child, and I was a stay-at-home mom. I started talking to my parents again, and I felt I had to have a relationship with them. I stated I forgave them while sharing with my group, but then why am I so angry? They were still toxic, trying to control me, and I didn't want to feel all this anger and resentment that hurt me again. I didn't know what to do; do I keep this fake relationship, or do I just cut it off?

Time passed by; I was about eight years clean; at this point, we went back east for a holiday, and when we got there, something felt way off. I couldn't deal with the feelings, so I slept most of the time. I hated it there, and the same feelings as a kid returned. He came to my room and asked me to talk, and my father told me he wanted me to call everyone in the family and tell them he didn't abuse me. I said I couldn't do that because it was not true, and then finally I said what I needed to say for so long.

He stated that I was going to raise a hostile child and I was not parenting well, and you call yourself a Christian? What type of program was I in that was not working? And what a horrible person I was. I stood up and said: "You know what these programs showed me is that I don't have to put up with this. I know the truth". Then I grabbed my family, and we left, and I felt good. It had been so long, but the truth was out, and I felt a weight lifted off my shoulders. It felt good that I stood up for myself and said what I had to say. I cut all ties with them; no social media, no calls, no texts, no emails; I blocked them from all of our phones. And that's all I knew; I was running, disappearing, and isolating. This was my coping skill.

But I was so confused about how to feel; I was angry again, depressed, and just wanted to sleep all the time. I stopped attending meetings and church and just wanted to be in "my blur."
Some of the guys that worked for us went to bible study and a program called Celebrate Recovery, and I saw a change in them but still, I wanted to feel miserable. They also started going to a step study. What are the 12 steps and religion? They would explain it to me, and we would talk about it before work started. I went a couple of times when the tattooed pastor would teach. I kept seeing the change in these guys. Their change intrigued me, and one day my husband said there was another step study opening and asked if I wanted to start one. I said no and kept saying no because I was not done being miserable.

He asked one more time, and I finally said yes; I believe it was God saying pick yourself up and stop feeling sorry for yourself, and I went kicking and screaming the whole way there. I knew what to say with these questions they were asking, so I answered them, which was glorious and professional. The step study leader said I want to know what you think and feel; well, you asked for it, so I let it all out in my answers. Then something started happening within me, and the misery was leaving me, and my mind felt lighter. My answers were so long because I have held in that misery for so long. Later, I was baptized at Canyon Ridge Christian Church; Jesus washed all my sins away, and He forgave me. Now it was time for me to forgive.

It was years since my parents, and I had had any contact. After completing the 4th and 9th steps, I wrote an amends letter to them (I didn't send it), but I let everything go that was my part in my life situation with them. This step changed everything started changing my heart to warmth and compassion again. I can see again the weight that has been weighing me down for my whole existence. I can't believe how alive, and well I feel today. I could finally see, and breathe, and the pain in my body was less than before. I even sent my parents an email and a text message. Communication has started slowly again.

I was getting into the Word of God, into the healing of myself through Christ's light. One day my father sent me a letter apologizing for his actions. The Holy Spirit worked hard in my life, and I felt HE was doing this miracle for sure. The more I got into scripture and trauma healing, "the blur "went away. After four years of no contact and not seeing them, we finally met when I was back east visiting family.

Now in this new life of mine, I began seeing, and feeling emotions, and being ok with feeling whatever comes up, and how to work on the negative feelings, as well as working through them. The greatest gift is that I give back today as a leader for the Spiritual Care Chaplaincy Program and Chaplain at WestCare Nevada that I serve with.is that I give to a homeless ministry that helps people with trauma, addiction, and mental health disabilities. The forgiveness of my trauma let me genuinely begin to love not only myself, but others and to love them for whomever they are.

✝

Chaplain Michelle Hatter

Michelle is a self-published author through Eagle Authors, a Christian Based publishing company. Her first book is called, "Braiding Session."

For 40 years Michelle has called Las Vegas her home.

When she is not working at Las Vegas Care Center as a Medical Records Assistant, she spends time with her Diva Granddaughters, Natalia, age 8 and Victoria age 5. In her spare time Michelle likes to design Christian tee shirts.

Michell is also a Chaplain with MOFM and loves serving God's people. She also teaches a women's bible study in her church.

Michelle is currently in the process of writing two children's books, one is called "Can You Say Granny? and God Sees Color."

† Forgiving What You Can't Forget
By Michelle Hatter

My fondest memory of my mother was when I was four years old. She was standing on the porch waving goodbye to us as we left the John D. Shields Projects, where we lived. My grandmother and grandfather were picking us up for church. She wore a beautiful yellow sundress. A yellow silk scarf, the same color as her sundress, was tied in a bow around her short brown hair. Her cocoa-brown skin against the yellow sundress made her one with the sun. She was so beautiful to me, almost like a princess. As she stood on the porch waving goodbye, I watched her out the car's back window, not wanting to let her out of my sight. That Sunday, I just wanted to stay home and stare at her in that yellow sundress. I wanted to tell her how much I loved her.

As I got older, something changed. I never saw my mother with those innocent young eyes again. When the person who is supposed to love you and nurture you tells you that you will never be anything in life, you start to believe it. That's what my mother would say to me. When you hear it so often, you begin to think about it yourself. I became that person she told me I was. I was nothing, and I would never amount to anything.

I loved my mother, but I never liked her. I always thought she felt the same way I did; she loved me but never liked me. The older I got, the less my mother and I got along. I realized that, for whatever reason, my mother was unhappy. As a little kid, I thought her unhappiness was my fault. Some days, she could not function without having a drink. I didn't know what the word alcoholism meant when I was younger. As I got older, I realized it was a disease. I also learned it is a cover-up, a coping mechanism to get her through the day and what was really going on in her life. Today, my mother would be considered a functioning alcoholic. She cared for her family; she could cook and clean like nobody else's business. She ensured that her children and my father were taken care of.

I wanted to prove her wrong when she said those things to me. But in my mind, I thought she was right. She had to be right; she was my mother, who knew me best. All I needed was her love and validation. All I wanted was for her to say how beautiful and smart I was. I wanted her to tell me that I would be something one day. I wanted her to say how proud of me she was. Those words never came. So, I went seeking validation from other places. I sought validation from young boys and men. They told me what I wanted to hear. I was too young to understand that they only told me those things to get what they wanted from me. Finally, I became pregnant at sixteen, seeking the validation I needed.

Years later, my mother and I became friends. I was still seeking her approval, needing her to tell me how much she loved me. We never talked about it. My mother died of cancer without giving me the things I thought I needed to become a woman. I did not know that despite my age, I still needed answers.

Have you ever had one of those "But God" moments? All the Sunday school lessons and going to church with my Grandma Mittie and her prayers could not have prepared me for what God had for me. I started to seek Him, the Lover of my Soul. God is so good. One day, God revealed some truths about my mother. It was mind-blowing truth. I was sitting in my car, wishing my mother was there with me. Sometimes a young woman needs her mother's advice. That day, I just wished she was there. I needed the hug—the touch only a mother can give her baby to soothe the pain. I needed her love. Somehow, I thought her presence would make my problems disappear. When my son was younger, and he got a boo-boo, all I had to do was kiss it, and miraculously, it would all be better. I needed that miracle kiss from her. I needed answers. I needed her motherly advice. My mother died of pancreatic cancer in 1977 without telling me the secrets of life. The things that I needed to hear.

I sat in my car crying uncontrollably, like a baby wanting her mommy; my heart was broken. I wanted to die. I didn't want to live anymore. I wanted my mama. I called out to God. "I need you, Lord. I need answers that only you can answer for me." "But God," is all I can say. I love Him. His grace and His mercy are overwhelming. In the book *Jeremiah 29:11, it says: "For I know the plans I have for you," declares the Lord, "plans to prosper you and not to harm you, plans to give you hope and a future."*

The awesome God that He is has ministered to my heart. His Spirit sat next to me in my car and spoke to me. He told me that it was a generational curse. My grandmother told my mother the same things that she had said to me. My grandmother never told my mother that she loved her. Instead, she told my mother that she would never be anything in life. She said to her that she would always be a failure. It was the exact words—the words my mother said to me were the same as those my grandmother said to my mother. And my mother never felt love from her mom because my grandmother's mother told my grandmother the exact same things that I had heard all my life, the same words that my grandmother had said to my mom. Generations of women did not know how to encourage their daughters. My mother had wanted the same thing from her mother that I had sought from my mother, and my grandmother had wanted the same thing from her mother that we all wanted and needed: love, worth, and validation.

God said that I would be the one to break that cycle. I had to break that family curse of loveless women. I had to do it for my son. And so, I would love on him every day when my son was young. I would tell him and show him how much he was loved. I would say to him

how special he was to me, and that God created him just for me to be his mom. My Father, My God, also showed me how gifted my mother was, and He told me I was a lot like her. He told me that she loved me, but she didn't know how to say to me or show me because she was never encouraged by her mother. My heavenly father told me that the drinking covered up the pain she was feeling. My Lord ministered to me that morning, sitting in my car. God goes beyond the things that we could think of or even imagine.
Ephesians 3:20 says: "*Now to him who is able to do immeasurably more than all we ask or imagine, according to His power that is at work within us.*"

My father opened the heavens and showed me my mother's face. She spoke to me. She told me how proud of me she was and that I was a good mother. She told me that she loved me. My mother was smiling. Her face wasn't riddled with pain but joy and pure peace. It was the face that I remembered when I was four years old. Tears covered my face. My heart was full of the same joy. My tears were of appreciation and adoration for my heavenly father.

God didn't have to do this miracle for me, but He did it anyway. That day, I realized the extent of God's love for me. His grace and mercy endure forever. I thanked God for the power of forgiveness. I forgave my mother, I forgave my grandmother for my mother, and I even forgave my great-grandmother for myself, for my mama, for my grandmother, and all the women in my family. Jesus broke the curse for my son—and now, for my granddaughters.

Chaplain LaVenia Davis-Sandoval

LaVenia Davis-Sandoval loves big hair and bright colors. She is a wife, mother of 5 and grandmother of two. LaVenia comes from a long line of entertainers. She is the great-granddaughter of Earl Campbell who played trumpet with Count Basie and Louis Armstrong. She is the favorite and oldest daughter of Chicago's own Blues Singer Katherine Davis. She is a singer, an actress and writer. LaVenia has toured Italy twice, Canada the Bahamas, Israel and 30 US states mostly as a performer and some just out of love of travel. Some of her performances include acting in television commercials, Children's Theater, musicals, and stage plays. LaVenia is classically trained by the late Dr. Maria D'Albert of the Sherwood Conservatory of music to which she performed as a Coloratura Soprano with the Hungarian Opera Workshop. She also studied voice with the Great Dr. Lena McLin also of Chicago which prepared her for different genres of music.

Some of her performances include but are not limited to The JW Pritzker Pavilion, the Lyric Opera House of Chicago as well as lead and background vocals on digital recordings. LaVenia is an ordained chaplain serving in the city of Las Vegas and is a firm believer that what happens in Vegas goes all around the world. LaVenia has spent her most recent years feeding and clothing the homeless on the streets of Las Vegas Nevada. She is currently serving in the Ministry with children at the International Church of Las Vegas.

† True Forgiveness Is of The Heart
By LaVenia Davis-Sandoval

Forgiveness is a 12-year-old me reaching through the iron bars of Cook County jail (assuming he ever got caught) to tell the man who took my virginity that I forgive him. Forgiveness is necessary. True forgiveness is of the heart. Forgiveness takes the heaviness off by freeing you from its stronghold. It does not mean the other person gets off "scot-free" it simply means that you are not bound by it.

Everyone has gone through something. Everyone has a story to tell. Here's mine. I had been praying for all of those girls at Michigan State who had been assaulted by that evil doctor. Having been a victim of rape myself I was relieved to know that justice was being served. When I was visiting my mom in Chicago is when I first heard about how he had assaulted over 200 girls. I began praying and asking God to reveal every demon harming our children. Seemingly in an instant I got a call from my oldest daughter Safari. I could taste the saltiness of her tears through the phone. "Momma, your son is sick!" She proceeded to tell me that my oldest son Prodigal had molested his younger sister Amber some years ago. It started when she was 5 and he was 11. I felt so sick to my stomach. So many thoughts ran through my mind trying to figure out how such evil could have entered our family. These are things that you hear about in other families. I believed Amber but I needed to talk to Prodigal. It was then that I learned he had been molested by cousins when he was younger. My stomach sunk even further into what must have been my soul. Having been a single mother of five children I did everything possible to protect my children. I didn't want what happened to me and Safari to happen to any of my other children, so I thought that keeping Amber home with her brothers was the safest place.

I remember being safe when my mom came home one night and swung the front screen door of our home open and said, "get out!" I don't know what I did or what any 12-year-old could do to be put out on the streets of Chicago. I didn't have any money so I decided to walk to my friend Vince's house to see if perhaps he had 50 cents so that I could ride the CTA bus to my grandmother's house. I rang Vince's doorbell and he said he didn't have any money and insisted that I hurry up and leave before he got into trouble. At that point I knew I'd be walking to my grandmother's house. It had to have been around midnight because it was 11:40 when I left my mother's. I knew I could do it because I had taken this 3 hour walk many times before. The only thing was that it was always during the daytime.

Before this night happened, I would say that these were good times growing up on the southside of Chicago. We had so much fun growing up as kids playing games like hide and go seek. So many places to hide, such as in your neighbor's yard or in the alley. We were 3rd generation growing up on 79th and Loomis where everybody knew everybody. It was like one big family. You were free to run around all day as long as you where home before the streetlights came on. Late night was very different. not many cars on the road nor were their people moving around. It didn't matter though because I knew how to get to Grandma's.

About 15 minutes from Vince's house, I turned around almost instinctively but I only saw a beautiful Crescent Moon and somebody's mutt lapping up water from a leaky fire hydrant that I'm pretty sure the neighborhood kids were playing in earlier that day. I took a few more steps and then suddenly my mouth was covered, and both of my arms were behind me with a knife poking me in the back. I was then lifted off my feet and whisked into the alley. I Never saw his face, but I do remember the skeleton and crossbones tattoo he had on his hand. To this day, I don't see what's so fashionable about brands with skeletons on them.

I quickly spiraled into a depression. I didn't want to live anymore so I made lots of unsuccessful attempts at suicide. I felt alone and unloved. As with a lot of girls who become rape victims, I became promiscuous. I just wanted to be loved but I found myself in more vulnerable situations. I can recall times when I would reach out to so-called friends seeking emotional support only to find myself unclothed again and even more numb. These were male friends who took my cry for help as an opportunity to have sex with me.

At age 15 I met 18-year-old Xavier. For the 1st time I'd finally found someone who loved me. Not knowing then that what I was seeking was already inside of me. It is the father's love to which no fleshly love could ever compare. Early into Xavier and my relationship I became pregnant. In my 15-year-old mind that simply meant having a big stomach. I remember seeing girls at school with big stomachs and then they'd leave school. I didn't want to leave school so when my mother asked if I wanted to keep it or have an abortion, I chose the latter. I kept hearing that it's just a fetus and my being too young to understand that it was actually a baby growing inside of me. I showed up to Planned Parenthood, signed some papers, laid on the table and listened to that dreadful vacuum literally sucking the life out of me. I literally killed my baby. Depression continued to have its yoke around my neck until 5 years later when Xavier and I had Safari. I vowed I would never kill another baby. Motherhood was my happy place. I figured the most important thing a child needed was love and I had plenty to give.

I was 30 years old when I realized I was still ensnared. While running errands with family one day, we pulled up to a stop light and I started hyperventilating and crying uncontrollably. Once I was able to maintain my composer, I realized we were just around the corner from where I was raped when I had the panic attack. I had been married for 5 years and was the mother of 3 children. By now I had performed overseas as a singer and actress and was involved in the things that I was passionate about. My life equated to holding a ball under water. As long as your hand is there, it'll stay submerged. The moment you remove your hand that ball will pop up. You may not see it but it's there.

One day there was an elderly woman at a crosswalk waiting for the light to change. She was carrying 2 large bags, so I offered to help her carry them across the street and she gently smiled at me and replied no thank you. I smiled back, the light changed, and I proceeded to cross. Before making it to the curb I saw nearly a hundred more bags waiting on the other side. This precious woman would carry 2 bags a short distance then goes back for 2 more until she gets them all together then starts the process all over again. To this day I wonder what was in all of those bags. For me, any form of unforgiveness would be synonymous to what this woman was doing. You have a destination in mind but each time you reach back you can only get so far.

I knew I needed help. After being counseled by Pastor Barnett of Living Word Christian Center in Forest Park Illinois, I took it to the altar and laid it all at the Fathers feet More importantly I left it there. Soon after I felt inspired to get baptized a 2nd time. I'll never forget the warmth that came over me. I was born again, a new creation. Old things have passed away. Behold, all things are new. That old person had died.

I am so happy that I was smart enough to seek counseling. I could have continued on with life as usual. Having it together on the outside but inside shattered and broken getting into random altercations, always feeling the need to protect myself because I couldn't that night. People tend to blame God in tragic situations but *John 10:10 reminds us that if it steals, kills or destroys it's the enemy.* How often have you heard I can forgive but I can't forget? True forgiveness is of the heart. You have to let God into those secret places to cleanse you and uproot the things, but have you bound. Unless it's destroyed at the root it will continue to produce fruit.

I think there's a fear of that person getting away with the offense in terms of forgiving, but you heap coals of fire onto their head when you do. This takes the weight off of you and places it on that person so to speak. The Bible says if you have any unforgiveness in your heart that You cannot ask the father for ANYTHING. As I forgive, I am forgiven. It's no coincidence that what happened to me also happened to my children. These are generational curses. Because I was able to forgive my offender, I could freely ask forgiveness for those I've offended. Now I can intercede for my children and my children's children by binding every generational curse and loosing a hedge of protection around everything attached to me.

In Luke 23 and 24, Jesus said *father forgive them for they do not know what they are doing.* He was the perfect example of how we are to treat those who have wronged us. *Do not let the sun go down while you are still angry. Ephesians 4:26* Don't sin by letting anger control you. I am so at peace. It's a peace that surpasses all understanding. I look nothing like what I've been through but rather what Jesus has done for me at the cross. Forgiveness is possible. My smile, my sense of humor and my inner peace all reflect my Daddy. I've always gone to church, but my relationship is so tight that there's nothing that the enemy can do to separate me from His love. Now my life a reflection of who He is; the Great I am. Haggai referred to Him as El Roi, the God who sees. The disciples asked who sinned that this man was blind at birth. Was it the parents or the baby? Jesus makes it perfectly clear that it was neither, but He is the one who brings the healing. Let Him heal you today. Trust Him with your bonds of pain. He knows what you're going through. He knows the pain that you've been subjected to. What happened to you and even the hurt that you've caused does not define who He created you to be. Let Him do for you what He's done for me.

Everything within me wanted to run rather than write this chapter because it exposes deep dark family secrets. I would equate it to opening up an old wound after decades of it being stitched together. The sweetest words I could ever hear in this moment were from Chaplain Tamia when she said, "Show up like Jesus showed up for you!" No one is to blame. Certainly not my mother. Her father had just died; husband had just walked out on her leaving her a single mother with 4 daughters at the young age of 28. With tuition for private school, mortgage on a new home and a car note on a new car.

Today she's a loving mother, grandmother and great-grandmother to her children and loved by her fans who know her as Blues singer Katherine Davis.

I bow before you in total surrender. I don't know why this has happened, but I know that only You can uproot these seeds that the enemy has sown. I recognize that I am not what happened to me, but I am who God says I am. I am not the mistakes that I have made. I am who You say I am. That makes me whole, and complete. Cleanse me of all unrighteousness. I rededicate my life to You giving you my all. Nothing is greater and mightier than You, the Alpha and Omega. You created the heavens and the earth and everything within it and nothing and no one can stand against the God of our salvation. I thank You Father for showing me how to forgive as You have forgiven me for my sins. Show me how to love in spite of… I thank You Father for hearing me for You've always heard me. I love You and thank You for loving me 1st. In Jesus name, Amen

†

Chaplain Ingmar Joel Njus

Ingmar spent the first nine years of his life on a farm with no electricity or running water in northern Minnesota. In 1948 his family moved to Compton, California. He was active in the Boy Scouts and achieved his Eagle Award. He graduated from Compton High School and enlisted in the Naval Reserve. He obtained his BS degree in secondary education (mathematics and physics) from the University of Utah and was commissioned an Ensign in the United States Navy June 1962. During his 24 years on active duty, he served several tours off the coast of Viet Nam, received MS degree in Physical Oceanography from Naval Postgraduate School, taught College Algebra and Introductory Oceanography at the University of Hawaii extension division on Midway Island, and studied Economics and Political Science at the Navy War College graduating with highest distinction. He retired as a Commander. His awards include the Navy Commendation Medal and Defense Meritorious Service Medal.

After retiring from the Navy, he was Chief Financial Officer at Get Graphic, Inc. in Vienna, Virginia, for two years, and later moved with his family to Las Vegas, Nevada. After 26 years with the US Postal Service, he retired (again) as a Supervisor on March 31, 2020. Earlier that month his youngest son, Michael, lost his battle with cancer and July 1, 2020, his wife of sixty years, Leanne, went to be with the Lord. He, his daughter Kathryn, and son Kevin still live in Las Vegas.

Ingmar has been a lifelong Christian. While growing up in Compton, he was active in St. John's Presbyterian Church. He was president of the Student Christian Fellowship Group at the University of Utah and Protestant Lay Leader on his first ship. He is currently a member of The Four Seasons Church in Las Vegas. Since becoming ordained as a Chaplain with the Messages of Faith Ministry, Nevada Chaplaincy program on November 5, 2021, he has volunteered with the Hope for Prisoners 100 Christmases program, participated in a missing children search with Nevada Child Seekers and Free International, and is actively involved in RECAP (Rebuilding Every Community Around Peace) Program. He is continuing to build his faith and develop his goal of providing service to others while pursuing additional courses through the Nevada Chaplaincy training program.

† Forgiveness Is Letting Go
By Ingmar Joel Njus

Having experienced many thefts, break-ins, and vandalism over the years, I would like to be able to say, as Jesus did when they nailed Him to the cross, *"Father, forgive them for they know not what they do" (Luke 23:34),* but it is difficult to think that those who were committing the crimes did not know what they were doing at the time. It is often said that what you see in others is what you have in yourself. Growing up in an era when we never bothered to lock our doors, it is hard to imagine someone doing thousands of dollars in damage in order to steal a few or even a few hundred dollars of personal items. It was devastating, but it was just material possessions. Fortunately, no one was ever injured - God's blessing.

Identity theft, home invasions, burglaries, and vandalism were all done by unknown perpetrators. The hate and anger I had toward them was a total waste of time and effort. It had no influence on any of them. They were not even aware of it. The only one being hurt was me.

The identity thieves that struck several years ago were very professional. After using one of my credit cards accounts to transfer a few thousand dollars to a new account and opening new charge accounts at several businesses and merchants around town, they placed our phone on call forwarding so we were not even being notified when these new accounts became delinquent. Frustration followed, as the police appeared to take no interest in following up on any of the leads that we had uncovered and provided to them. Fortunately, the banks and affected businesses were either able to recover some of the stolen money or they wrote off the losses that they had incurred. We were at least made whole financially, but the animosity lingered for a long time.

A few years ago, some bad guys struck again. This time it was much more serious. While we were out of town for the weekend, thieves broke into our home and stole jewelry, money, credit cards and anything of value they could easily carry off. My daughter came by to check on the house while we were gone, and apparently interrupted them. As she entered the front door and turned right to see why the lights were on in the dining room, indications are that the intruders quickly and quietly came from the other end of the house, sneaked out the front door, and ran down the driveway, dropping items as they left. Fortunately, there was no confrontation.

Two days later they returned to finish the job. They ripped the plywood off the boarded-up window and carried off computers, laptops, televisions, stereos, a bicycle, tools, frozen food, kitchen appliances, silverware, etc. In the process, the house was totally ransacked. Our home was uninhabitable at that point, so when we returned home, we moved in with my daughter.

All was quiet for a week. Just when we thought everything had settled down and we had begun to make plans for cleanup and repairs so we could move back in, they struck again - and again the following day. Even with my son, my daughter, and me watching the house twenty hours a day, they managed to break in every day for a week during the brief intervals we weren't watching. The last two occurred even after we installed a monitored alarm system. During this time, they continued to carry off or damage anything that was left. On some occasions, when we came by, we would find trash bags and plastic storage bins packed full and pre-positioned for later pick up. Sometimes they would be outside the back door, by the gate to the back yard, or even just stacked on the front porch.

As each shattered window and battered door was boarded up, they would select a new point of entry. By the time the break-ins were over, they had broken out four windows and smashed in four doors. Every shelf had been wiped clean and every drawer pulled out and dumped. You could not walk anywhere in the house without stepping on or climbing over something. It looked worse than any hoarder's house. Cosmetics, hair dye, shoe polish, ink cartridges, food coloring, drink mixes, coffee, and other food items had been emptied, broken open, or stepped on. As a result, nearly all the floor coverings throughout the house had to be replaced. Total repair costs for damage to the house approached $100,000. Thankfully our homeowner's insurance covered most of the repairs. Some of the stolen or damaged items were also covered by insurance, but the monetary compensation in no way replaced the sentimental value or compensated for the trauma and stress involved.

We had lived in that house for almost thirty years following my retirement after 24 years in the Navy. Having been married nearly sixty years and with my visits to numerous places on five continents, our family had accumulated a lot of souvenirs and memorabilia. Nearly a lifetime of accumulated "treasures," including family heirlooms, all my medals, awards, and navy uniform items, were all gone or destroyed. There were many irreplaceable items such as my daughter's charm bracelet reflecting a lifetime of memories, jewelry I had given my wife on special occasions, and going away gifts she had received from many of the duty stations where we served.

Was this just a reminder from God of his warning in *Matthew 6:19- 21*, to *"Lay not up for yourselves treasures upon earth, where moth and rust doth corrupt, and where thieves break through and steal, but lay up for yourselves treasures in heaven, where neither moth nor rust doth corrupt, and where thieves do not break through and steal, for where your treasure is, there your heart will be also."* Had I been concentrating on the wrong treasures, and was He trying to redirect my priorities?

The best way to overcome the losses is to not focus on what you lost, but to focus on what you have left. It does no good to dwell on past events that cannot be changed. Everything could have been so much worse. God's timing is awesome. He made sure we were not around when the break-ins were taking place, or the few times that there could have been serious encounters, He kept our family safe and unharmed.

Only once did we encounter anyone in the house. One afternoon when my son stopped by there was an intruder near the back door. When my son came in the front door the individual shouted, "Oh, ####" (expletive deleted), and bolted out the back door and over the block wall in back. By the time my son (who is almost six feet tall and 220 pounds) made his way through the rubble and to the back door the guy was gone. We lost a lot of "things," but fortunately at the time, we still had each other, and we still had the memories. Thank you, God.

There was an outpouring of support and offers of help from friends and my co-workers at the post office when they found out about the situation. My co-workers even went so far as to research my service history and obtained replacement medals and ribbons and presented them to me in a beautiful shadow box. What a blessing it is to know that others still care and are there for support when you need it the most.

One of the "bad guys" was eventually arrested and went to prison.

At his sentencing he had nothing to say, and he showed absolutely no remorse. He had been apprehended while the police were serving a warrant on him for another burglary, and at the time he was on house arrest and wearing an ankle bracelet while awaiting trial on a previous burglary. He was sentenced concurrently on all three burglary charges. I recently received a notice of his request for early parole on his own recognizance, so he could "go back to school and better himself."

I responded, "absolutely not." He had been out on his own recognizance before, after committing one burglary and continued to burglarize and vandalize other homes at that time, even while wearing an ankle bracelet. I thought he should be kept locked up for as long as possible to protect other homeowners in the area from possibly being subjected to the same invasion and trauma. I look back and, after some soul searching and prayer, I wonder if my response was really an altruistic concern for my neighbors or was it an opportunity to have revenge and retribution on him. I do not know what the feelings in his heart were. Was he truly looking to improve himself, as he suggested, or was he only looking for an opportunity to return to his old ways? I don't know the outcome of his request. I can only pray for my forgiveness for any ill feelings I may have toward him.

We need to be sure to differentiate between the evil and the evil doer. Just because you forgive someone, does not mean you condone what they did. As the Psalmist said (*Psalms 97:10*) *"Ye that love the Lord, hate evil,"* but as Paul wrote in his letter to the Church at Ephesus in Ephesians 4:32, *"Be kind to one another, tenderhearted, forgiving one another even as Christ forgave you."* I need to pray for him, let go, and move on, knowing that his forgiveness is between him and God.

I was recently hit with another vandalism attack where, in the dead of night, a vandal cut all the copper piping from my home's hot water heater and air conditioner and removed the batteries and copper battery cables from my motor home. I want to ask, "Why me Lord?" *but I know the Lord says for every season there is a reason (Ecclesiastes 3:1).*

Over the years there will be lots of trauma in your life. Some will be physical, some verbal, and some emotional. Some will be very real, and some may just be imagined. The best advice I can give is to confront the situation and try to forgive as soon as possible. The longer a bad experience or an unkind word is allowed to linger, the deeper the anger grows and the more the resentment builds. Remember, the only one it hurts is you. Many times, you are your own worst enemy. As John Lockwood Huie said, "forgive those who have injured you - not because they deserve your forgiveness, but because you can never be happy until you release your anger and grant forgiveness." From this it seems clear that the benefits of forgiveness favor the person forgiving perhaps more than the person being forgiven.

Remember too that forgiveness is a two-way street. Not only is it necessary for you to forgive others, but you must also search your soul for any hurt that you may have caused others to suffer. You must be equally as quick to ask for their forgiveness. It is amazing how this small act can generate an enormous amount of good will and lasting favorable feelings.

Just as others may not be aware of how badly they have hurt you, sometimes you may not even know that you have offended others. Take inventory of your relationships. Have some of them turned cold or ceased to exist? You need to ask if you have inadvertently done something to cause this separation. If so, an apology and asking for their forgiveness may ease the tensions and restore a harmonious relationship.

Forgiveness is not always about trying to make someone else feel better but is about being able to let go of the hate and anger you feel toward them, or in the latter case removing the animosity they feel toward you. In either case, forgiveness, in the final sense, is between you and God. The end result is knowing that you have done the honorable thing and that you have a clear conscience and a pure heart. Forgiveness is knowing that you have restored a loving relationship, not only with others, but with your God.

Saying "I'm sorry" is easy but letting go is not. Forgiveness, however, is only half the story. The other half of forgiveness is forgetting. There are always memories or trigger events that bring back those feelings of hate and animus. God has promised us that He will never give us more than we can bear and for every problem He offers a solution (*1 Corinthians 10:13*). *To get rid of the hateful feelings, they must be replaced with something else. That something is love.* He has commanded us in Mark 12:31, and Paul reminds us again in *Galatians 5:14, "thou shall love thy neighbor as thyself."*

It seems exceedingly difficult to love those that have hurt us or stolen from us, but with God's help it can be achieved. We cannot love others if we don't love ourselves. We can only experience this kind of love if we have the love of Jesus within us. You cannot both love and hate something or someone at the same time. The hate needs to be replaced with love.

The answer then is turning the problem over to God, asking Him to take your burden and replace it with love. It is not our place to withhold forgiveness from others. As we read in *Matthew 6:14, "For if you forgive other people when they sin against you, your heavenly Father will also forgive you."* God forgave us, so who are we to not do the same. True forgiveness is not just saying "I'm sorry" and moving on, but is really about being more loving, forgetting the hate and trauma that we have suffered, and letting go.

✝

Chaplain Beatrice Dyess

Beatrice was a member of True Love Missionary Baptist Church under the leadership of the late Pastor I. W. Wilson. On Thursday July 12, 1979, she was baptized and filled with the Holy Ghost at Pentecostal Temple COGIC. In 1995 she was licensed as Nevada State Evangelist. Evangelist Beatrice Dyess founded several ministries; mainly "Voices of Experience", which was to provide a platform for the pioneers to share their true- life experiences.
She is an anointed prayer warrior, with the gift of prophesy, intercessory, teaching, conducts workshops and prayer shut-ins. Evangelist Dyess also founded Prayer Warriors Uniting for Christ; Self Discovery Workshops; skits, plays and youth explosions, which only are a few that she implemented in Las Vegas, Nevada.
Beatrice Dyess was born in Tallulah, Louisiana to her late parents Horace and Elizabeth Moore. Along with her mother and siblings they moved to Las Vegas, Nevada in 1951, where she attended school and graduated from Rancho High School. She graduated from Las Vegas Cosmetologist and worked in that capacity for a few years. Later began working at the El Cortez Hotel as a change girl, while waiting to be hired by the Clark County Sheriff's Department. This truly was her dream career. On May 5, 1969, Beatrice Dyess was sworn in with the Clark County Sheriff's Department. After the City of Las Vegas Police Department and the Clark County Sheriff's Department merged, on 8-11-1974 she was commissioned as a Police Officer with Las Vegas Metropolitan Police Department. She attended the police academy 9-8-1974, along with four other females, and graduated 12-6-1974. She states that they were the first females to attend the academy to be assigned to Patrol. This fulfillment of one of her dreams, bestowed the honor on Beatrice Dyess as becoming the first Black female officer in the State of Nevada and the first Black female Officer with LVMPD. What an honor. While working in the Youth Diversion, one morning Beatrice heard the Lord say to her, "fill out your retirement papers, I will take care of You". On 8-8-1997 she officially retired as the first Black female officer with the LVMPD.
Beatrice Dyess is the proud mother of 4 children; Michael, Angela, LaTonya and Akili; 13 grandchildren and 12 great grandchildren.
In 2007 she graduated with a General Associate Degree from CCSN; 2017 received her Doctor of Divinity, D.D. with Kingdom Builders Bible Seminary and on 5-14-2022 she was ordained as a Chaplain with Chaplaincy of Nevada.

† **Forgiveness Is the Ministry of Reconciliation Manifesting In Me (Us), Through Me (Us), For Me (Us)**

2 Corinthians 5:18-19 All this comes from the God who settled the relationship between us and him, and then called us to settle our relationships with each other. God put the world square with himself through the Messiah, giving the world a fresh start by offering forgiveness of sins.

On October 16, 1978 while sitting in the waiting room at Valley Hospital, Beatrice Dyess and family were informed by the doctors that they would not be able to do anything else for Elizabeth Moore, the mother of Beatrice Dyess and her then remaining four siblings According to the doctors the severe stroke that her mother had, there were only approximately five other cases. who had suffered a severe stroke and there were only five other reported cases. It was at this time that she committed her life to Jesus Christ and made a commitment to him, "that if he spared my mother's life, I would serve Him the balance of my days". Her mother's life was spared, and Elizabeth lived until April 29, 1988.

The Ministry of Reconciliation takes place in a context of brokenness- the broken relationship between God and humanity, the distortion and destruction of the bond between humanity and the rest of creation, brokenness in the area of human relationships and often brokenness in the church, Genesis 3:22, Romans 5:12, Isaiah 59:2.

Due to my (our) broken relationship, *Isaiah 59:1-2, with God, he sent his son Jesus Christ to die on the cross, Mk. 15:21-41, Romans 3:23, 1 Peter 3:18, Eph. 2:13, John 3:16, is the basics of my (our) forgiveness and justification. By grace through faith, I (we) are no longer enemies, ungodly sinners or powerless. God's love has been poured into my (our) hearts when I (we) repented and accept Christ as our Savior, 2 Cor 5:17, Ro. 5:5* Thus, I became an ambassador and must exhibit that same love, care, and concern for others by allowing the Holy Spirit to manifest the operation of The Ministry of Reconciliation in me (us), through me (us) and for me (us). I (we) am learning to love God enough and have compassion on fallen humanity and present the message of salvation to all without respect of persons, acts 10:28-34, Ro. 2:11. Thank the Lord for his mercy and patience with me (us).

Those that I (we) am alienated from as a result of sin against (me (us) and God through injury, abandonment, abuse, vicious wicked acts, rape spiritually or physically, the message of peace, love and forgiveness must be demonstrated through me (us) to them. Whatever has caused relationships to soar, and a wedge driven between us, definitely calls for the act of forgiveness, Matt. 6:14-15, Mk. 11:25, Mt. 18:21-22, Eph. 4:29-32, 1 Jn. 1:9, Pro. 20:22, Lk. 6:31 on my part and yours.

Let us look at the definition of reconciliation. Reconciliation is Christian Theology, an element of salvation that refers to the results of atonement. It is the end of the estrangement between God and humanity which was caused by sin. Another definition for reconciliation is the process of two people or groups in a conflict agreeing to make amends or come to a truce. God reconciled all of creation back to himself through the death of Jesus, Ro. 3:25-31. In order to be reconciled, it requires us to put our faith in Jesus and believe the word of God, Phil 2:13 and *Phil. 4:13 reads, I can do all things through Christ which strengthens me.* It is not of myself or yours, but through the strength and power of the Holy Ghost that I can, but we must cooperate with him.

God does not expect me, neither you to put ourselves in harm's way when a heinous crime or offense has resulted in trauma or destruction to us or a loved one. For instant rape, murder, or abuse etc. we are not required to establish a relationship with such individuals, however for peace of mind I must seek the Lord that I (we) might be endowed with the courage and grace of God to forgive the offenders that I (we) might be free. Think about it; I (we) minsters reconciliation to others and they go free, but when it comes to myself or you, it will be a shame to remain a prisoner to unforgiveness. On another note, in situations that occurred Lord I pray that you give me (us) the grace and help from God to forgive myself (yourself). The word of God reveals to in *Romans 12:19-20, Dearly beloved, avenge not yourselves, but rather give place unto wrath for it is written Vengeance is mine; I will repay saith the Lord, v20-Therefore if thine enemy hunger, feed him, if he thirst, give him drink; for in so doing thou shalt heap coals of fire on is head, v21, Be not overcome of evil but overcome evil with good.*

I (we) cannot afford to stay in the place of unforgiveness, even though I (we) have a right to feel the way I (we) do, having been violated through no fault of my own. I will not sabotage or destroy my own destiny. The offender is not worth destroying my (your) life and future regarding any incident that may have occurred to cause me or you injury mentally, physically, spiritually, emotionally, or financially. Of, course I have to pray and use wisdom as to who I should embrace. I will not allow anyone to put me on a guilt trip anymore. When the act of reconciliation will cause additional damage or bondage to myself (or yourself) or others, by all means we must restrain from future contact with that individual. But I must release them sincerely from my (your) heart by forgiving them which does not mean that they are free of the offense but that I (you) can move on with my (your) life and place them and the situation into God's hands.

Have you heard the statement, "Hurting people hurt people" and "if it's in the root, it's in the fruit." If unforgiveness remain in my (our) hearts, it will cause hurt to those I (we) love and care about. Some hurts and damaging situations may require the aid of a counselor in order to forgive and be healed. Healing belongs to me (you), to us, Ps 30:2, and Ps 147:3 reads, *He healeth the broken in heart and bindeth up their wounds. I would like to share a testimony at this time.*

Many years ago, my ex-husband was involved in an extra-marital affair. We eventually separated and divorced. I really thought I had forgiven both of them however, one morning I attended a prayer service and to my surprise, the female came into the service. The conductor of the service knew her and requested that she read a scripture to which she did. The members of the church gave her many accolades. I could feel unforgiveness, jealousy and hatred began to surface in my entire being and at the same time I was shocked that I still housed those emotions of sin. I thought within myself "the audacity of her to be there and to have the members compliment her, only compounded the ugliness within me. I felt as if I was unsaved and a hypocrite. All that day at work, I repented and sought the Lord for healing within me of the unforgiveness. I don't know when he actually answered my prayer but when I returned to the church the next morning, she was there and after prayer, thanks be to God, I was able to embrace her with love and forgiveness because the Lord had anointed me with the spirit of forgiveness.

I could not do it on my own, but it took the Holy Spirit working in me his will and the doing of his will, through me crying out to him to purge me, heal me and deliver me from the sin of unforgiveness. The Holy Spirit manifested his love and power in me through me and for me that I might be able to forgive her and others. Many other sins had attached itself to unforgiveness because I had not released it to God. In *Phil. 2:13 reads for it is God which worketh in me (you) both to will and to do of his good pleasure. Mt. 6:14-15 for, if ye forgive men their trespasses your heavenly Father will also forgive you. V15 -But if ye forgive not men their trespasses neither will your Father, forgive my (your) trespasses.*

Forgiveness is.......The Ministry of Reconciliation manifesting in me (you), through me (us) and for me (us). Thanks be to God and all the glory belongs to Him. In Jesus' name my Lord and Savior.

†

Forgiveness Is
Life Changing Stories from Las Vegas Chaplains

copyright@CN2022

Made in the USA
Las Vegas, NV
01 December 2022